THE
MARK

PAUL YADAO

ALL RIGHTS RESERVED
COPYRIGHT: © 2012 PAUL YADAO
ISBN: 978-0-9830980-8-9
LIBRARY OF CONGRESS CONTROL NUMBER: 2012937092

I dedicate this book to the Triune God of Love, the Father, the Son and the Holy Spirit, Who has marked me and blessed me with every spiritual blessing in the heavenly places in Christ and chose me in Him before the foundation of the world, to walk holy and blameless before Him in love.

To my loving parents Tatay and Nanay. I am always proud to be called your son. You have taught me the value of family, serving, and loving others unselfishly.

To the fathers and mentors of my growing up years in the Lord who have left an indelible mark of blessing on my life through the years.

To my spiritual dad, Leif Hetland. Thank you for believing in me. I am a living testimony of the transformative power of the Father's blessing. I was released into my destiny and call to bless the nations the day you bestowed on me the mark of the Father's Love.

To Ahl, my beloved wife, and our two wonderful children, Dave and Sophie. You are God's testament that I am indeed God's bull's eye of love, goodness and favor. Every moment with you is priceless.

To our sons and daughters in the Lord and the whole Destiny Family, heaven is a living experience here on earth because of what you do and who you are.

To the generations to come, whose exploits and ex-

periences in God would be far greater than ours, and whose sacrificial love will finally cover the whole earth with the knowledge of the glory of the Lord just as the waters cover the sea. This book is for you.

Contents

6 | MARKED

20 | WITHIN REACH

37 | THE NAME

53 | THE SEAMLESS HEART OF GOD

68 | FACE TO FACE

86 | MARKING OTHERS

108 | BLESSED

120 | EPILOGUE

CHAPTER ONE

Marked

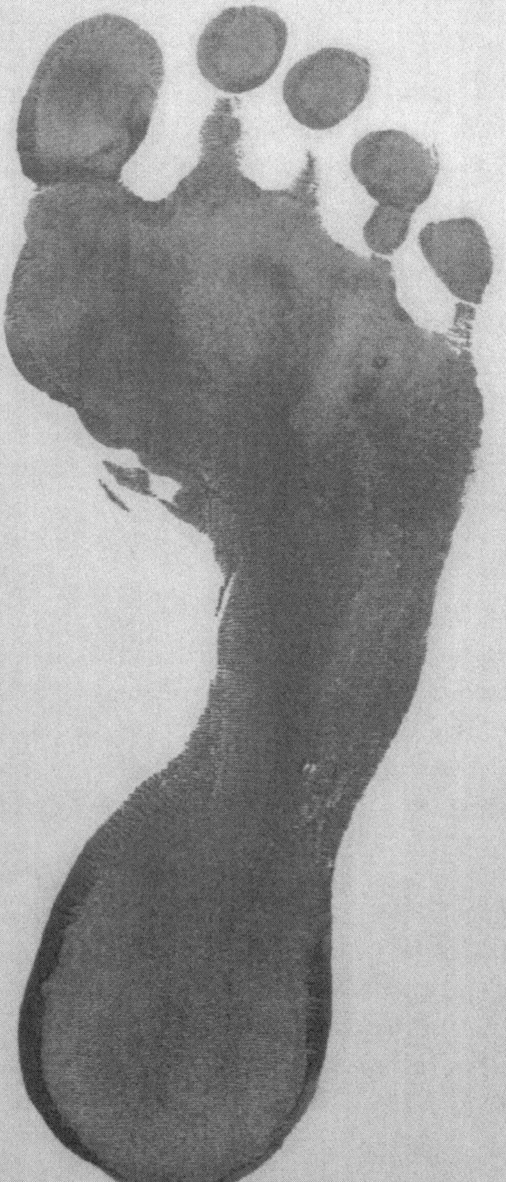

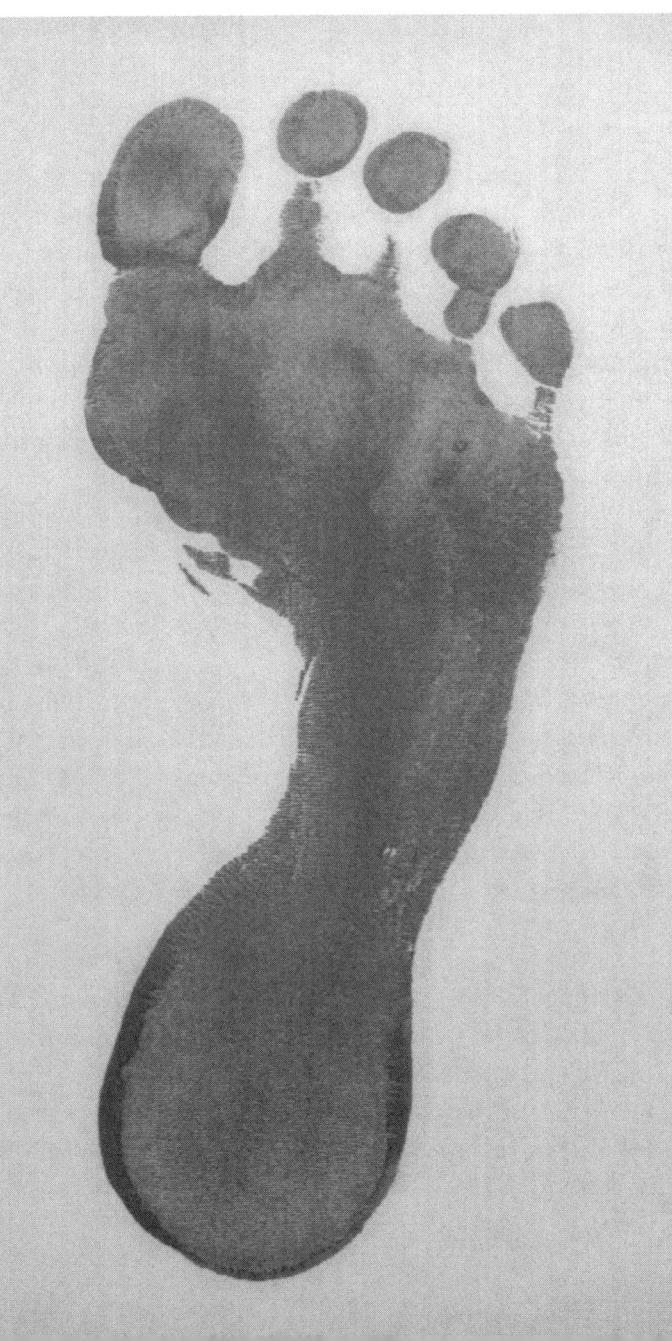

DUSK. *In the faint glow of the fire, his mother sat on the ground choosing among threadbare tunics. All her other precious belongings had been bundled in a sackcloth. Which one tunic would she carry with her in the journey to a 'promised land'? All these, once vibrantly colorful garments, had sheltered her from the scorching sun and swathed her from the terrifying whips of the Egyptian guards. Now, she must choose only one.*

The past days had been horrendous. He had been digging by the river when the water turned scarlet and overflowed with dead, bloated fish. He shuddered at the memory of frogs, gnats, and lice. He could still smell the stench of dead livestock in the evening air. It seemed as if the whole land had been cursed and doomed. But what bewildered, yet terrified, him most was that he and his family had remained unharmed. "Were they next?", he wondered. Would the same God who sent horrible plagues to Egypt spare bondsmen like them?

He had seen the holy men, Moses and Aaron, gathering all the families of Israel. He heard them proclaim that the time was near; that the God of Israel would come and rescue His people from the yoke of slavery. He heard them assure Israel of deliverance and hope long buried under the burden of toil and slavery.

He felt his belly churn as he heard the hurried clamor in the kitchen. His father laid a thick piece of meat on the fire. The meat was seasoned with salt and bitter herbs, as was the journey that his family was about to embark. This uncharted journey towards a land they had only seen in their dreams promised freedom, but also threatened leaving the only life they had known. The new, strange land was a promise they had bitterly struggled to believe in through the years. Moses said that only one more sign would have to be demonstrated, the sign that would finally impel Pharaoh to let them go. There was no doubt that this would be the most dreadful of them all.

His father called for him, jolting him out of his thoughts. "Go and fetch the pail from the slaughter. Hurry now!" He sprang up and ran to where his father had earlier sacrificed a choice lamb at twilight. As he scurried back, blood trickled over the sides of the pail, spattering on his bare chest. The pail felt sticky in his hands. His father commanded as he took the pail and smeared the blood, using a bundle of hyssop branches, on the door posts.

The final hour had come.

In silent haste, they sat and ate. No meat, no un-

leavened bread, and no bitter herbs were left uneaten. As the night grew, no one dared to say a word; they merely found comfort by huddling side by side. For fear of an eluding hope, they nodded off together in each other's arms.

MIDNIGHT. *The rattling shutters woke them as the wind howled. In the far-off distant there was a growing lament as grief-stricken women had gone loose in the streets wailing for their lost husbands. The unsettling fear grew within them. Yet, as the weeping continued, they realized that the impending sound was not of mourning lovers, but of moaning mothers robbed of their children.*

Wretchedness, darker than darkness itself, swept over Egypt, leaving no man room for solace. Death had visited like a thief in the night.

Pharaoh's voice thundered across the expanse of the palace. But it was not the loud scolding familiar to bewildered servants. It was a deep, agonized bawl that sent the most powerful man in Egypt begging on his knees. He entreated every sorcerer in Egypt, presenting each one immeasurable wealth in exchange for the resuscitation of his son. Each magician called upon his gods, straining every hair and fiber for his cries to be heard. Incense, magic dust and stale potions filled Pharaoh's senses, yet his son remained limp in his arms. Not knowing where to channel his grief, he ran aimlessly around his bastion carrying the lifeless child. Pharaoh pressed his own chiseled face to his son's babyish skin, hoping that his own breath might awaken this innocent boy smitten by his father's unbreakable will.

Gnashing his teeth and bruising himself, Pharaoh whispered, "Let them go." When his servants did nothing, he let out an embittered roar, "Drive the cursed brutes out of my kingdom at once! Let the Jewish slaves go!"

Fumbling in the obscure morning light, the Jewish emissary ran as fast as his legs could carry him. With Pharaoh's words still ringing in his ears, he echoed the message of deliverance to every Jewish household. The words that his own tongue carried left him dazed, and in disbelief, he would occasionally slap his wrist, if only to assure himself that he was not in a dream. As his eyes saw the first morning light, they brimmed with hot tears for it had just dawned on him that the words he spoke were the very pronouncement of his own liberty. In awe he wept, no longer a bonded messenger, but a free man, heralding at his own behest the thrill of his own emancipation. He was free!

DAYBREAK. *Only when the sun rose did his family gather enough courage to peer outside their house. His father yanked the door and ran to his brother's house. He ran to his nephew's house. Then to his cousin's house and to his comrade's house. He returned panting, throwing his arms in the air yelling, "We are safe! We have been saved!", they shouted in exuberance and danced around the house, crying with elation, "The Lord Almighty has spared us! He has heard our cry!"*

Not long after their exodus from Egypt into the promise land began, while the cities of Egypt sulked in bitter, accusing tears; the villages of the Jews overran with gladness. People danced in the streets and sang resounding praises to God. Awe and delight overwhelmed them as the Egyptians offered generous amounts of clothing and jewelry. The very people who forced them into adversity were now freely giving them favor. God had not only delivered them, but also blessed them.

On that day, Israel experienced something they had never known before, unspeakable joy. In the midst of surrounding calamity, an overwhelming peace blanketed the people of Israel.

The blood of the sacrificial lamb had spared Is-

rael. But the love and fondness of the Almighty liberated them. God did not just protect Israel, He set them apart.

He bestowed on them the MARK OF BLESSING.

Many significant marks and symbols have defined history and shaped our society. There is the cross, the swastika, the crescent moon, the national flags, and many others. As individuals,we perceive these marks differently. If we have experienced being in a war, the mark of the Red Cross gains utmost importance as it implies emergency aid and health care. But if the only battle we have experienced is the daily traffic as we commute to work, or finding a place to eat at two in the morning, then coming across a green light or the golden arches of McDonald's can be much more momentous than sighting a red cross!

There is such a thing called God's MARK OF BLESSING. In the same way, the significance of this mark is in accordance to its relevance to us. If you are utterly content with your life today, with your family, career, ministry, and outreaches, then this message will most likely go in your right ear and exit your left. But if you **hunger** for more of the move of God in your life, if you are not content with your present situations, if you know that there is more to life than what you see and experience every day, then this book is for you.

"An act or word of approval, conducive to happiness" that is how my Merriam-Webster dictionary describes blessing. However, in the Bible, blessing is defined better—**it is the bestowal of supernatural favor.**

This supernatural favor is vividly illustrated in the stories of the Passover and the Exodus, which account for God's ultimate redemption. The horror of the plagues, the euphoria of the exodus, and the miracle of the parting of the Red Sea grips and moves us to marvel at God's power.

But we can draw another assurance from these stories. God was actually showing us that **His very Word and promise, when proclaimed over our lives, serve as a seal, a cosmic mark that commands the whole universe to align for our good and for His glory.**

When the Lord laid this message upon my heart, He led me to Genesis, the very first book of the Bible where it all began. Even then, God shows us the vitality of blessing. God made everything perfect. He made man perfect, but if you notice, after creating Adam, Genesis 1:28 says:

*"Then God **blessed** them [man] and said, 'Be fruitful and multiply. Fill the earth and govern*

it. Reign over the fish in the sea, the birds in the sky, and all the animals that scurry along the ground.'" (NLT, emphasis mine)

It was after **declaring blessing** that God gave Adam his assignment to rule over creation.

Abraham's story of how God called him and promised to use his offspring to bless the nations, also speaks of the mark of blessing:

[1]"Now the LORD had said to Abram: 'Get out of your country, from your family And from your father's house, To a land that I will show you. [2]I will make you a great nation; ***I will bless you and make your name great; And you shall be a blessing...***"
(Genesis 12:1-2, NKJV, emphasis mine)

God did not literally give Abraham sons. None of his children suddenly fell from heaven. Instead, God declared His promise to him, and Abraham acted on it.

Abraham did great things because God chose him to be a target of His blessing. I doubt that he was singled out because of his supernatural good looks or his eloquence. Likewise, the Israelites were not the most grateful or optimistic, or even the most prayerful of people, but they were God's elect. Why did God have to go to such drastic measures to demonstrate His favor to these clueless, undeserving men? He had to have something up His sleeve!

I think that God, lavish as He may be, did not do this just to spoil Moses and the Israelites. He had a purpose that would outlast them all. **He marked them for blessing and for His purposes.** The frightened, forsaken, and forlorn Israelites, who knew nothing but hardship, suddenly became a singing, rejoicing lot ready to conquer the unknown. They became who they were because someone (in this case God Himself) professed blessing over them, making them the bloodline of many chosen generations and fulfilling God's promise to Abraham.

Slaves became freemen. The cursed became favored. The hopeless became eager and spirited.

Do you need that kind of turn-around blessing in your life today?

Are you defeated?

Are you bitter from years of fruitless labor?

Are you living a mess of a life?

Are you sad, lonely, afraid?

Are you undeserving?

Do you have peace?

Does your faith falter?

If you believe that there is so much more to this life than tedious routines and wearisome mediocrity, then I have good news for you.

The supernatural favor that God gave to the Israelites is still as potent and as accessible today as it was then. The God who sealed the Israelites with goodness has not changed one bit. These stories in the Bible serve as an invitation for us to step into that same realm of favor.

If deep inside you there is an ache to be the person you know you were meant to be, or if you want to discover the great destiny that God has for you, read on. Abraham himself had no idea how or when

God's promised blessing was going to unfold. Neither did he get a money-back guarantee in case His obedience would lead him to uncomfortable times. But he believed nonetheless. The only thing that outweighed his belongings was his faith and his willingness to see God's promise through.

As we read and claim these principles in our own lives, let us unravel a mystery that God has so affectionately hidden for His children – the mystery of His divine mark of blessing. Let us together experience the stirring adventure that God is about to take us on!

A Moment with the Almighty

Dear Lord, thank you for the wonderful destiny you have planned for me. I come before you as I am—with my doubts, my imperfections, and my fears. Help me to lay down my burdens so that I can receive the blessing you have so lovingly intended for me. I open my heart and come to you as a child, expectant to hear you and know more about your heart for me. In humility I position myself so that I too can be a target of your divine mark of blessing. Amen.

CHAPTER TWO

Within Reach

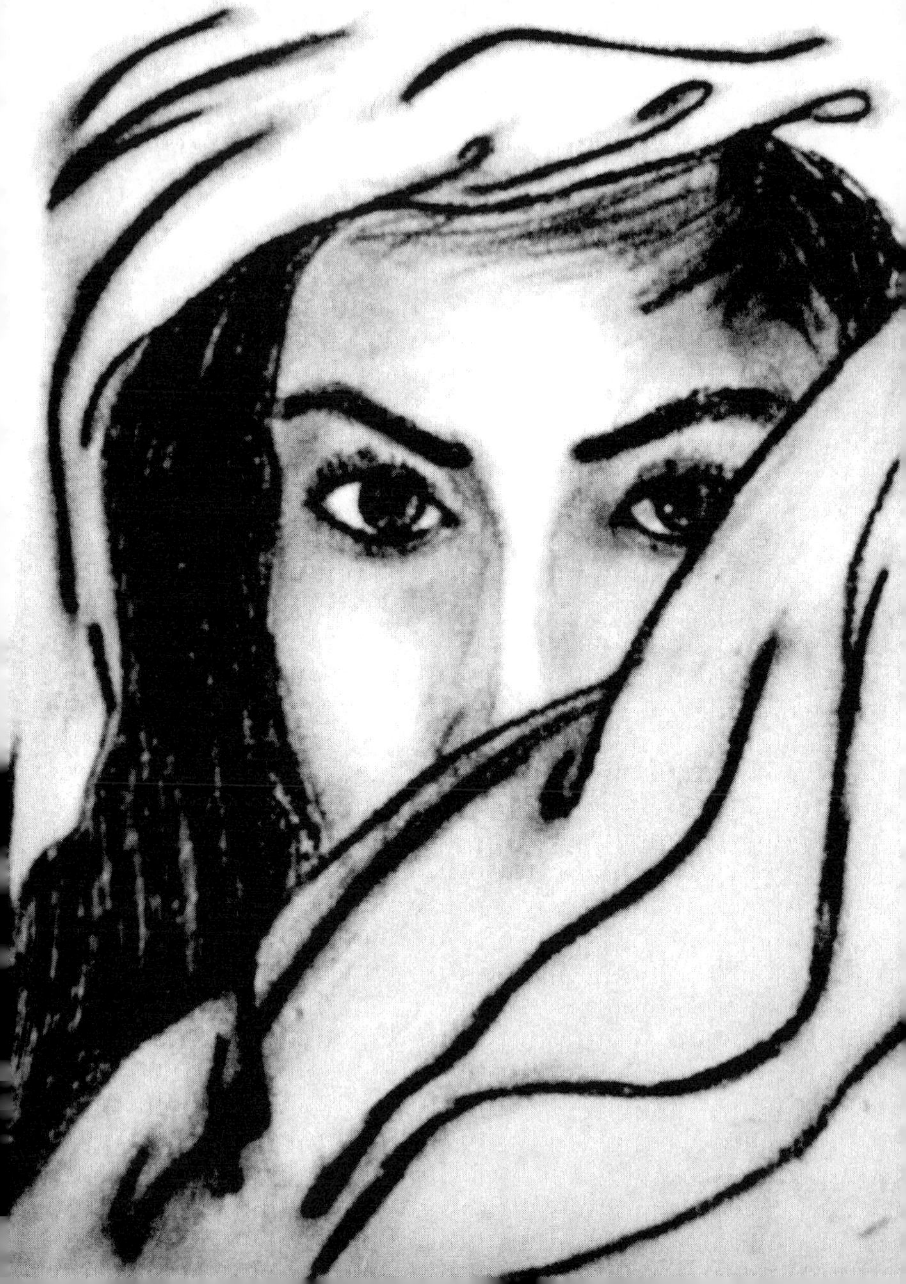

Have you experienced gut-wrenching pain of scorn, disheartenment, and rejection? Well, you are not alone.

There are people who have faced disappointment, discouragement, and even disillusionment at many points in their lives. Thomas Edison was scorned by his teacher as being "too stupid to learn anything", yet he later patented over a thousand inventions, including our modern day light bulb. Michael Jordan was pulled out from his high school basketball team, yet he is now hailed as one of the basketball legends of all time. Walt Disney was fired by a newspaper editor because he "lacked imagination and had no good ideas," but then we all know who Walt Disney is now, right?

These modern-day heroes shared two things. First, they had a burning dream. Second, they were all constructively stubborn. They sure paid the price in trying to reach their goal, but they chose to disregard all the name-calling and create for themselves new labels of willful persistence and deliberate breakthrough. They knew there was something they just had to get their hands on.

Have you ever felt this way? Have you ever

wanted something so much that it literally hurt you? So much that the aching you felt in your heart made you think that your chest might just burst open at any moment?

Such was the case of a woman named Hannah[1]. Hannah was in love with a man named Elkanah. While she was also the apple of his eye, she, unfortunately, was barren and could not give Elkanah any children. Being barren at that time was the ultimate cultural stigma for a woman; it implied her failure of being a real woman.

Then Hannah had to contend with Peninnah, her husband's other woman. Peninnah was cruel and she was jealous of Elkanah's steadfast love and obvious favor towards Hannah, despite her barren womb. Thus, Peninnah pestered Hannah with condescending and snide remarks at every possible occasion. Her greatest insult was that she, Peninnah, had been blessed with a fertile womb and could give Elkanah a child.

Imagine Hannah's shame and torment, as well as her constant battle against self-pity, resentment, misdemeanor, and retaliation. Imagine her conscious painful effort to refrain from being offended by God for closing her womb. The bittersweet hassle of motherhood was something she deeply longed for. Every single day Hannah waited eagerly for her miracle with a driving desperation in her heart.

It was in these grueling times that Hannah developed great emotional fortitude and an almost violent faith in God. She endured this time of hardship because the magnitude of her desire for God to intervene was so much greater than her need to be justified before men. She had learned to trust God's goodness, and every mockery she heard fortified her faith. Instead of living in a perpetual self-pity, Hannah decided to use her desolation as fuel for intercession.

One particularly agonizing day, when she could no longer take Penninah's verbal attacks, Hannah turned to God. She fled to the temple weeping for the Almighty to give her a son, making vows in exchange for that gift. Yet, there in the temple where she sought refuge, she received even more mockery. In Hannah's desperation, she was mistaken to be drunk by the high priest, Eli, and admonished to get her act together. What a godly woman she must have been not to have lashed out on that person who had just openly rebuked her in her place of worship.

All the years of anguish must have mounted up at that moment. That insult from Eli could have been the "straw that would break the camel's back." But Hannah was totally transfixed on God. Hence, the devil's supposed blow seemed like a slight jab to her armored heart. No scheme of the enemy, and certainly no insult of man, could be odious enough to take Hannah's eyes off of God.

Hannah responded to Eli with respect. Aware that he was a priest and questioning him, would be like questioning God's purpose of putting him in the temple. Questioning God was a concept utterly unbefitting of Hannah. Her heart had been kneaded and primed for this defining moment. With feet adamantly anchored in faith, Hannah was entrusted with a blessing that only someone like her could competently steward.

After benevolently explaining herself, Eli realized his mistake and responded by saying, "Go in peace! May the God of Israel grant the request you have asked of him" (1 Samuel 1:17, NLT). Eli spoke blessing to Hannah, and she went off a happy woman. Hannah's curse of bareness was broken by her humility and desperation, yet it was Eli's mark of blessing on her that finally unlocked the door of blessing in her life. Though Hannah had yet to see her son, her deep faith once again prompted her to count the spoken Word as its very fulfillment. Hannah knew she had laid hold of her breakthrough, and in that assurance, every bit of sorrow left her. Her once ashen face was now radiantly aglow, warmed by the thoughts of a little baby that she would soon bear. She must have waltzed joyously back home, gliding along the dusty path as if it grew with new grass.

To Hannah was born Samuel who would become one of the greatest prophets in the Old Testament, a prophet after God's own heart. Samuel was holy and esteemed; a real man of wisdom, yet he was humble and compassionate in spite of his exalted stature. He was much like his mother. Samuel entreated God with as much fervor as a barren and aching woman would, except that the prize he sought was God's lingering presence.

Hannah had become a fulfilled woman because of Samuel and the sons and daughters who were born after him. These children were the fruits of her womb, the joy of her abundant household, and the embodiments of her steadfast faith.

If there is a lesson we could single out from this

story, it is that spoken blessings find their target in hearts that are ready to receive. 'Blessing' comes from the root word *beraka* which means to 'kneel down'. It speaks of a posture by which we are able to receive it—humble and adamant against offense. Greater blessings are given to those who have the heart to capably steward them, and the faith to remain expectant until the promise is fulfilled.

We may not be as impeccable as Hannah. We may not have the capacity to face offense head-on and emerge victorious. But we do have the same God as she did—one who dreams of greater things for us; one who wishes for us to realize that trials are nothing more than a way for our capacity to be increased. We have the same God who promises the grace and power for us to see the promise through blessings and curses

BLESSINGS AND CURSES

When we hear the word curse, the general public may tend to think of it as a verb with this mental image: @*#$%&!. Cursing is one of the big no-no's we teach our kids. When others hear that somebody has been cursed, it forecasts visions of witches clutching pin-covered voodoo dolls. While this may be partly

true, let us re-define what a curse
refers to a curse (noun) as "a praye
harm or injury to come upon some

Concisely, a curse is the opp
In essence, if we do not have the
our lives, we are consequently living a cursed life.
This life is not necessarily of unexplainable pain or
anguish, but it's a life that is devoid of a favor that we
are meant to possess and thrive in!

God has a great destiny for each one of us.
Though it is great to be happy with what we have and
to be comfortable with our lives, we should never
stop growing until we live and breathe that very life
of fullness promised to us in His Word.[2]

Allow me to share my own story of blessing.

THE TURNING POINT

May 2006. My wife, Ahlmira, and I had been
invited to participate in a mission consultation at the
Hosanna Lutheran Church in Lakeville, Minnesota.
After the consultation, we found ourselves so privileged to be attending Randy Clark's School of Heal-

We hadn't planned on attending, and, frankly, I was not so familiar with what it was about. But no doubt, it was a divine set up. God had something big planned for us.

Not having a clue what to expect, our hearts pounded in anticipation to hear from God and to experience Him in every session. We were so desperate for a fresh encounter with Him. At every opportunity and at every altar call, we came forward to be prayed for. You see, we were at a particular season in our lives when we needed something new from heaven, something that would propel us into our divine destiny.

I had been in the ministry for almost sixteen years, and my wife for about ten years. I started out as one of the leaders of a campus ministry called the Students for Christ (SFC) in the early nineties. This student-based movement at the University of the Philippines in Los Baños, the national state university in our country, later gave rise to our church, Destiny Ministries International. Through the years, we saw God move powerfully in the university, saving and transforming lives of countless students. We experienced major moves of God that touched the campus and later on spread to different provinces and campuses nationwide. We were so radical for the things of God! In the year 1998, we were sent to Malaysia to serve the Lord there as missionaries.

After all these breakthroughs, we experienced what seemed to be a protracted season of wilderness. Two years into our work in Malaysia, the season in our sending church shifted. The ministry we left in the Philippines went into a major 'molting' season. We were called back home to help put things back in order.

At that time, we did not know what was in store for us. Somehow, we felt that we had been displaced, pulled out from our ultimate call to spread the Word to the nations, and instead to take up a cross that was not ours to carry. It scarred us deeply. Our firstborn, Dave, was barely three months old. I think that was the most trying time in our lives as individuals and as a family. But we obeyed. We left everything in Malaysia to start our old life anew.

With the burden for the Malays still burning deep within us, we did our best to run the local church in the Philippines. Yet, our efforts seemed futile and our personal ministry seemed lackluster. The years of service had taken its toll. We strived and applied everything we learned through experience in leadership to run the church, to no avail. Though giving up was not an option, we were tired and at the brink of burning out. We needed help...badly!

This is why we were at the edge of our seats during the School of Healing in Minnesota. Like Hannah, we felt such an ache and desperation within that we could've cared less about what others said, or what the odds were. All we knew was that only God, Himself, could help us. We were willing to get that help at any cost.

RECEIVING THE MARK OF BLESSING

In one of the sessions at the conference, Leif Hetland (Founder and President of Global Mission Awareness), preached a powerful message that intensely stirred something within us. It was the message on the Father's Love, and Healing the Orphan Spirit. Leif shared a testimony of his own encounter with the revelation of the Father's Love and how it radically transformed his life. At one point he mentioned orphan ministries and orphan ministers who are in the field trying to please God, much like the older brother in the Parable of the Prodigal Son.

I realized that I had been an orphan minister myself. Hence, I asked God to heal my heart and renew my mind. In an instant, I felt the love of the Father come upon me. It grew stronger and, finally, I came to a life-changing, heart-stopping, lightning-bolt-stunning revelation that He is indeed a Father to me and I am His beloved son through Jesus.

I felt so much freedom! The struggles I faced trying to work for God, and for the inheritance that He had already made available to me through Jesus, suddenly became clear. I knew this 'work-work-work-to-see-results' outlook had to go. Inheritance would be called wage if it had to be worked for. God was increasing my capacity by stressing that His promise was to be received and not earned.

Leif released a Father's Blessing to everyone in the room, a blessing much like the declaration of Father God to His Beloved Son, Jesus, when He said, "This is My Beloved Son in whom I am well-pleased". Those words totally rocked us to the core of our being, uprooting mindsets and attitudes shaped by an orphan mentality. The truth is that God is undeniably a Father, our Father, who loves every bit of us devotedly and without stipulation. What a moment it was; what a compelling revelation!

Adding to our already overwhelming God encounter was an event that would all the more transform our lives. Later in the conference, my wife and I asked Leif to be our spiritual father. As Leif accepted us into his spiritual family, we received yet another powerful impartation of the Father's Blessing. That covenant—that spoken blessing—released such tremendous favor and anointing over us as we had never before known in our lives.

THE FRUITS OF FAVOR

2010. It has been four years since that event. Within those years, God has been great to us in every way...family, finances, health, influence, anointing, ministry, etc., you name it! His hand moved in all these areas of our lives. The fruits of the blessing and favor declared over us in 2006 became fantastically tangible.

Moreover, the doors of opportunity swung wide open and the needed resources followed. From just one nation (Malaysia), prior to receiving the Father's Blessing, we were able to plant churches in Singapore, Cambodia, and Dubai. Through the ministry of Leif and our partnership with the Hosanna Lutheran Church, we have ministered in nations like Tanzania, India, and Pakistan. We saw major expansion in local and international church planting efforts. We saw mighty signs, wonders and healings. Along with these major ministry breakthroughs, we have also savored His goodness through material blessings.

Since we experienced the release of the Father's Blessing, we've released the same impartation to our spiritual sons and daughters. We've declared goodness and favor on many people at different situations in their lives, and, truly, we have seen their circumstances drastically transformed! In businesses, academics, families, relationships, and ministries, we've seen God's goodness flowing from one person to another. As the Destiny family has gone out to pray and release that blessing over people and over their realms of influence, God's favor has come upon them, as well. They've experienced blessing upon their health through radical healings; upon their finances through supernatural provision, jobs, promotions, salary increases; and upon their relationships through restoration and inner healing. More importantly, many have come to know and love the Lord.

The blessings that have poured upon our church would fill up volumes of books!

Once the blessing was given, people began to be released to the life of abundance that Jesus promised in John 10. Just like He did to Hannah, God marked us for blessing. Now that we have received the blessings, we will not let go! We look forward to seeing how the rest of our destiny will unfold.

Surely, He is not a partial father! He wants everyone, you and me alike, to be able to tap into that life of blessing and favor. Hannah is one of my heroes, and though my story is completely different from hers, I know God can move in my life in the very same measure. While this may be our testimony, it can be your story, also, because blessing does not choose time or location, just people who are eager enough to get hold of it.

Always remember that just as I received freely, I will give to you. As you receive blessing, may you have radical transformation in your life:

Our heavenly Father is faithful and true to His word! I declare upon you a mighty moving of the Holy Spirit within, to be able to see past offenses and hurtful situations and to forgive. I affirm the Lord's love and good intentions for you who believe and put your trust in Him. Just as the Lord has revealed Himself to us as a Father, I pray that the same revelation would come upon you as you read these words, to bring healing and deliverance, to commence forth blessing and favor, and to effect significant change in your life and community. May you have a posture that is ready for blessing – humble and ready to receive from Him. In the mighty name of Jesus, Amen!

[1] 1 Samuel
[2] John 10:10

CHAPTER THREE

The Name

What would your life be like if you were a professional wrestler? Not in the Olympics, but on entertainment television – donning fancy costumes and gripping viewers with over-the-top showdowns and exaggerated histrionics. What do you think your name would be—Vader, the Rock, the Undertaker?

Life would definitely be a blast! You would roll with money, fame, and power! Your face would be splattered on huge posters, and every time you walk in for a fight, fans would chant your name and cheer you on. It all sounds very appealing, except that the job literally hurts. Everyday on the job is a constant brawl, and you just might get your head smashed by a folding chair.

I think the tricky part would be the mask (and the skimpy costumes). The moment you step into the ring, you acquire a new identity. While that identity may bring fame and fortune, it will never be you. Any success you wrestle with will be attributed to your alter ego that will eventually die off when the crowds get bored. Life is not only a struggle, but also a pretentious game.

Wrestling entertainment was obviously unheard of in biblical times. But there did exist a man whose life, at some point, resembled that of a modern-day show wrestler. His name was Jacob, the Deceiver. In the peak of his wrestling career, he was known to have taken on an angel.

THE UNLIKELY CHAMPION

Jacob's life of struggle started as early as when he and his twin, Esau, were still in their mother's womb. Esau came out first, but when they delivered him, Jacob's hand was found firmly clasped around Esau's ankle. Jacob was born second and there, even before he spoke his first word, the quest to be first started.

From the day of his birth until Jacob grew up, he inwardly desired for the best part of everything. An opportunity came one day when Esau came in exhausted after a day of hunting. Jacob, with his scheming ways, tricked Esau into surrendering his birthright in exchange for a bowl of soup! Not only that, later Jacob would trick his blind father, Isaac, into giving him the blessing of the first-born, something that rightfully belonged to Esau.

Though deviously done, Jacob got a portion of wealth and blessing that he did not deserve. Along with these, Jacob got a brawny, angry, animal-hunting brother hounding him. Jacob's only option was to run away so he traveled far away where his uncle, Laban, took him in.

Laban saw Jacob's hard work and offered him wages for his hard labor. But Jacob had his eye on something else; more appealing to him than the earnings of an honest day's work was Laban's daughter, Rachel. He wished to marry her. So, for seven years, Jacob worked in Laban's land in return for the promise of Rachel's hand.

But this time, it was Jacob who would be deceived. At the end of the seventh year, Jacob asked for Rachel. However, in the darkness of the night, Laban secretly arranged for Rachel's older sister, Leah, to take her place in bed so Jacob would be forced to marry her instead. The morning came and Jacob was outraged. Jacob had apparently met his match! Jacob was forced to another seven years of unpaid service before he could get Rachel's hand in marriage.

Jacob was a skilled man, but more than anything else, he was street-smart. He knew that his years of labor for his father-in-law, Laban, would not benefit him as much as he would have liked it to. So again,

Jacob devised a scheme that would secretly allow Laban's livestock to become his own. When Jacob's assets grew, he took his two wives, their servants, his eleven children, as well as his servants, on the journey back to Canaan, his homeland.

As they traveled, Jacob remembered that fateful day when he escaped Esau and ran away with a life gained by dishonesty. The fear inside him grew, and he felt he had to appease the seething brother he might encounter along the way. He had his servants prepare an array of gifts—goats, donkeys, servants, and with it a message of humility to be given to Esau. Sure enough, his advance party met Esau. They presented the gifts to him and sent word to Jacob that Esau was coming with an army of four hundred men!

Jacob's knees wobbled.

He sent his family in different directions so some would survive in case they were ambushed.
With every step closer to Canaan, the tension grew. Anxious thoughts flooded Jacob's mind with a force much like the fury he imagined was running through Esau's veins.

All his life Jacob had struggled to make things

work to his advantage, sneaking around and manipulating for his own gain. That was what he did best. But now that he was about to face Esau, he knew he had no way around it. He had wronged Esau and knew that whatever would become of him, as a result of his trickery, was well deserved.

There was nothing to manipulate that would assure him of Esau's mercy.

There was only one person Jacob could rely on. If the slightest chance of gaining control over the situation existed, it would be to persuade God, Himself, to move on his behalf.

He needed to change God's mind. He needed great favor.

The match that challenged destiny.

Jacob looked around the empty camp. The bright night was shadowed by the fear in his eyes.

He sat on the ground.

Thinking.

Groaning.

Weeping until his eyes were sore.

He clenched at the dirt between his fingers. Then he looked up.

There a man looked down upon him, talking to him with a thousand silent words.

But Jacob's ears were deaf to consolation. His mind was clouded by his own deceit.

And so Jacob did what he knew best—he toiled.

He wrestled with the Angel of God until every ounce of his strength was exhausted.

Yet Jacob prevailed, with a strength he knew was not his own.

And as the first light of dawn broke the darkness, the Angel stopped.

But Jacob tangled himself in the Angel's form,

"I will not let you go until you bless me.

I WILL not let you go until you bless me.

I WILL NOT LET YOU GO UNTIL YOU BLESS ME!"

The Angel touched the hollow of Jacob's leg and left.

Daylight revealed a breathless Jacob, sprawled on the dusty clearing. Determined to get up despite the searing pain in his hip, he took a painful step.

Men saw Jacob walk with a limp. God saw a champion walk with purpose in his stride.

Jacob the deceiver was gone.

There stood Israel, a man of destiny. Prince of God.

RUINED FOR THE ORDINARY

If we read Jacob's story (Genesis 27-33) carefully, we would realize that God had actually given Jacob a promise, and Jacob even reminded God about it the night he was troubled with thoughts of Esau. Jacob pleaded with God saying, "...you promised me,

'I will surely treat you kindly, and I will multiply your descendants until they become as numerous as the sands along the seashore—too many to count.'"

Something seems a bit off—what was he still wrestling God for if God had already given him the blessing in the first place? In his head, Jacob knew God's promise well enough to recite it to Him. But in his heart, he lacked the faith and the confidence to believe in it. Maybe his circumstances and self-introspection had persuaded him to think that he needed to take matters into his own hands.

Jacob knew he was favored by God, but deep in his heart he needed to make things right. He didn't want to go on stage-managing every situation for his good. He so desperately wanted the continuous flow of anointing and favor from God, and he knew that only God could command these.

The Angel told Jacob, "Your name will no longer be Jacob...from now on you will be called Israel because you have fought with God and with men and have won."

Fighting and winning in a match against God does not mean that Jacob had overpowered the Almighty. Perhaps it means that despite Jacob's constant exertion against God, it was in the end, God's promise to bless Jacob that would not budge. Jacob had been set up. All his years of struggle, lies, and messy choices had actually been a prelude to this very night. His destiny was released through an encounter with God. Despite Jacob's frailty, he emerged a champion because what won was God's purpose for him.

Later that day when he faced Esau, the tides had turned. Instead of meeting him with a spear, Esau ran to Jacob weeping, overwhelmed by the reunion with his long lost brother. Jacob's encounter not only changed him, but also turned years of fear into a moment of bliss from this reconciliation. Everything in the past was forgotten, and, from then on, Jacob knew his days of deception were over.

Jacob had seen God with his own eyes, and that led to a radical change of perspective.

The place of fear had become a place of encounter.

He had been set free from the life of toil he had always known.

Yet, he gained a new identity—one professed by God.

So, for the first time, the works of Jacob's hands were borne in peace, for the sweetness of the presence and favor of God was upon him.

SEEKING TREASURES IN BACK ALLEYS

Before a man can set out to fulfill his divine destiny, he must first know who he is. To 'find ourselves', we try a lot of things. We hold retreats, getaways, and soul-searching sessions hoping to discover the person inside us and what that person wants. Sometimes, though, some of us struggle to find our identity in the wrong places—in our possessions, power, performance, and accomplishments. Like Jacob, we pour our efforts into endeavors that we think would shape who we are.

Yet from the life of Jacob, we learn that the best identity we could ever have is that which we find in God. We start to fulfill the destiny He has for us when we start to discover who we are in Him. The discovery of that true identity in the Lord is parallel to our coming and dwelling in the place of blessing.

It is in the presence of God—in the place of intimacy—where He bares His heart to us and shows us who we are and what we are capable of. It is when we hear the glorious voice of God, that we understand the difference we are to make in the world.

THE BEST ME

Our divine destiny is not solely defined by the extent of our service to the church, or the number of hours we spend preaching the gospel and discipling people. Rather, we realize our divine destiny when we become the best we can be.

If you are a teacher, then be a top-notch teacher! Artists, create with everything that is in you. Businessmen, use your hands to steward the resources God has put in your care. Parents, train your children well. Students, dedicate yourselves to learning!

We fulfill our divine destinies by excelling in anything and everything we do. We display the life of Christ in our lives, changing our communities and blessing the people around us.

Let us not limit ourselves into thinking that our destiny is locked away, hidden in a vacuum-tight vault. Let us, instead, change our perspective and believe that God has indeed chosen us for such a time as this—right where we are now. We have every opportunity to be the best we can be, for we are heirs of an extravagant God who revels in the triumphs of His beloved children.

We all have our Esau's—our failures, mistakes, and fears that haunt and hunt us, making us doubt if the promises and plans of God will ever come to pass. We also have our Jacob moments – we become overly introspective and feel insecure and condemned. In such a condition, we lose sight of God, we lose faith, and we lose hope. Our dreams die. Instead of feeling enthusiasm and joy, we feel burdened each day. Every season in our lives seem to be a hurdle towards a blurry resemblance of a happy life.

But we can also have our God encounters. That night in Peniel, Jacob thought he was wrestling for blessing. But in his wrestling, what dissolved was not God's unwillingness to bless him, but Jacob's fears and inability to receive the blessing.

All his life Jacob had programmed himself to strive for blessing, but in his God-encounter, he learned how to receive from God in a position of humility, trust, and total reliance on God. This encounter changed everything. It rid him of his fear; it gave him assurance of a life of blessing. Most of all, it transformed him into a brand new person – one who instead of straining for favor, came before God in surrender, finding his place in God and becoming the best man he could be.

Just as a prince cannot be secure in his identity as a royal heir without knowing his father, and just as he cannot effectively rule a kingdom without seeing his father doing so, we need to know God in such a way that we are confident enough to call Him father so that we can find our true identity!

We need to come before Him and seek an encounter that will propel us in the direction He wants us to go. This encounter need not to be a wrestling match like Jacob's, but it must have the same result. Like Jacob, we must realize that the great destiny God has prepared for each and every one of us is never a result of our might, but a blessing and overflow of the goodness and favor of God in our lives.

A Moment with God our Redeemer

Lord Jesus, we come in submission to You. Help us to realize our fears and to identify the things that hinder us from becoming who you really want us to be. We don't want to take our lives and circumstances into our own hands anymore. We want to embrace the destiny you have set for us. We want to encounter you the way Jacob did. We want our lives to change, so that we may be champions over every challenge that we face. Profess a new name over us, God! As we encounter more of you, may we shed all we thought we were, and may we see ourselves the way you always have meant us to be—as over-comers, as bearers of your blessing and favor. In Jesus' name, amen!

CHAPTER FOUR

The Seamless Heart of God

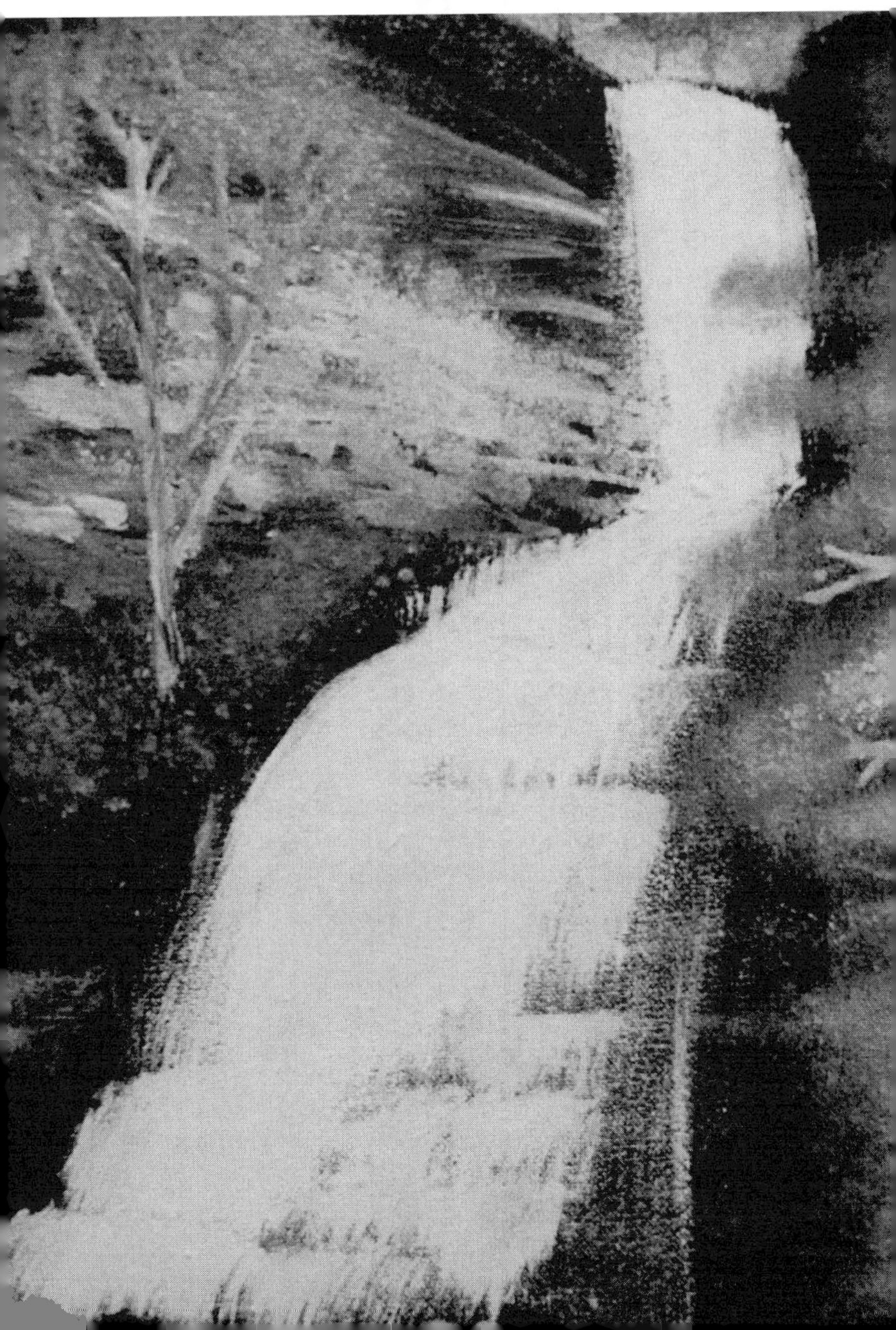

God never meant for us to figure Him out. An earthly mind attempting to fully comprehend the nature of God is like asking a three-year old to explain integral calculus—it's impossible! To say that we totally understand God would be to box Him into the pitiful limits of our carnal minds. While we may never be able to fully wrap our minds around His mysterious ways, we can have glimpses, and we can always, always behold His goodness and love, in its extravagance.

God is the greatest romantic there is. When we see lovers give big bouquets to their ladyloves, remember that it was God who created the rose bush. When we see people buy mansions and even islands to make their loved ones happy, remember how God told Moses that He would give him whatever land his foot stepped on? When our minds are restless and filled with the image of someone's face at the wee night hours, remember how the Psalmist describes God saying, "How precious are your thoughts about me, O God. They cannot be numbered! I can't even count them; they outnumber the grains of sand!" (Psalm 139:17-18a, NLT). Now we know who we take after, don't we?

The love of God may be kind and gentle, but it is

also jealous and unrelenting. It is a stubborn, do-or-die, kind of love that pursues us despite the countless drawbacks in our lives.

THE SANCTIONED MURDERER

Let's take a stroll through Genesis and explore the story of Abel and Cain, Adam and Eve's first two kids:

> *"...Now Abel kept flocks, and Cain worked the soil. ³In the course of time Cain brought some of the fruits of the soil as an offering to the LORD. ⁴But Abel also brought an offering—fat portions from some of the firstborn of his flock. The LORD looked with favor on Abel and his offering, ⁵but on Cain and his offering he did not look with favor. So Cain was very angry, and his face was downcast. ⁶Then the LORD said to Cain, "Why are you angry? Why is your face downcast? ⁷If you do what is right, will you not be accepted? But if you do not do what is right, sin is crouching at your door; it desires to have you, but you must rule over it." ⁸Now Cain said to his brother Abel, "Let's go out to the field." While they were in the field, Cain attacked his brother Abel and killed him."*
> (Genesis 4:2b-8, TNIV)

Cain was not an evil man. In fact, he was the first one who initiated giving an offering to God. If you read the verses carefully, you would even notice that Cain and God were on speaking terms; they knew each other.

Nevertheless, it was Abel's first-class offering that caught God's eye and Cain was anything but happy for his brother. I'm quite sure that if Cain would have just repented and given his best offering to God the next time, then things would have been alright. But Cain continued in the path of offense and consequently blamed Abel for making him look bad. In the end, he decided to get rid of what he thought was the root of his ordeal—Abel himself.

Now, let us consider how God handled the situation. When Cain was upset about the offering, God sought him out. God was not merely pointing out Cain's shortcoming or demanding for a better offering; He was explaining that Abel had done something pleasing that deserved affirmation (v. 7). God then counseled Cain not to sin by being offended and jealous of God's actions towards Abel.

Between the lines I imagine God was lovingly telling Cain that it wasn't the sacrifice that mattered to Him, but the heart of the one who offered it. Just as God desired for their parents, Adam and Eve, He wanted both Abel and Cain to be like Him—to be lavish in their expression of love and gratitude. While God's non-acceptance of Cain's offering may seem harsh, His heart was all good. He loved Cain and wanted to teach him, just as a father would his son.

However, Cain did not understand the heart behind God's admonition. He assaulted his innocent kid brother. Cain made a mistake, yet his actions did not change the way God approached him; it was still God who took the first step by seeking him out and asking Him where Abel was (Genesis 4: 9).

Of course, God knew where Abel was, but He asked anyway because He wanted to give Cain a chance to come clean, confess, and repent of his sin. In spite of this, Cain responded in denial and dishonesty, asking the famous lines, "Am I my brother's keeper?"

As the story unfolded, God punished Cain by cursing him to be a restless wanderer who would not yield the fruits of his labor on the land. It was a heavy sentence for Cain. Cain's parents, Adam and Eve, in their sin, caused the curse on man, and God compounded it by cursing the ground, as well. Upon hearing the verdict, Cain pleaded to God saying (v. 13b-14):

> *"...My punishment is more than I can bear. ¹⁴Today you are driving me from the land, and I will be hidden from your presence; I will be a restless wanderer on the earth, and whoever finds me will kill me."*

Though punishment may seem to be like a contradictory concept when we talk about God's love, we have to understand that punishment is the fateful result of another facet of God's character – justice. God is just. He could not help but be fair, and He displayed this impartial love to Abel by punishing the one who struck Him. Yet God did not let His yearning for Abel cloud His love for Cain, the murderer. God still loved them both in the same way. So in response to Cain's plea, God marked Cain (v. 15):

> *"But the LORD said to him, "Not so; anyone who kills Cain will suffer vengeance seven times over." Then the LORD put a mark on Cain so that no one who found him would kill him."*

Yes, you read it right. God showed His love to

Cain by bestowing a mark of protection upon him. In His holiness, God drove Cain out of His presence because He could not tolerate sin. On the other hand, neither could God tolerate that His beloved Cain would come to harm. In His mercy, God made sure that nobody would do to Cain what Cain did to Abel, defending him against the social stigma that we assume he deserved. There was no condemnation!

God's love is so bountiful that in it, even a murderer can be marked with blessing.

THE LENS OF LOVE

"How great is the love the Father has lavished on us, that we should be called children of God! And that is what we are!" (1 John 3:1a, NIV)

When the Bible calls us children of God, it speaks so clearly about how God loves us. Children do not need to do anything to be loved. Parents swoon over their babies' smiles and dedicate photo albums to their babies' first tooth. Children don't need to be saints or have college degrees for their parents to love them. There are no prerequisites for this kind of love because it is not based on deeds.

Luke 3:21-22 tells us about the baptism of Jesus. Jesus was thirty years old when John baptized him; Jesus was just about to start his ministry. Yet when He was baptized, God's voice was audibly heard from the heavens saying, "You are My beloved Son; in You I am well pleased."

Jesus had not yet performed a single miracle at that time—no walking on water, no preaching to the multitudes—yet God was already pleased with him! God already called Jesus His beloved Son.

Being described as children of God idyllically paints an image of the security and unconditional love we have in God. Yet, while this is true and very comforting, there is another part of the title that we often overlook, the 'of God' part.

To be of something means to be a part or product thereof. Hence, when we are called children of God, it does not just mean that we can find a place of refuge in Him. It also means that we are part of God's family. God expressed His extravagant love to us by sending Jesus, through whose blood we were counted worthy to be welcomed into His family.

It is through this lens of fatherly love that God

relates to all of humanity—as a perfect Father of the household who looks upon His children with affection, and desires nothing but the best for them.

THE HAND AND HEART OF GOD

We sometimes make the mistake of thinking that the hands and heart of God are interchangeable. A large number of people are offended because they do not understand the ways of God. In our lack of awareness we ask:

If God is all-powerful then why is there sickness and suffering?

Doesn't God understand that this is important to me?

Why doesn't He answer my prayers?

Why is He punishing me?

We whine and we kick; we see God's actions (or lack thereof) and judge Him at face value.

Let's take the fall of Adam and Eve. When they sinned against God, He punished them by cursing them and their offspring and by driving them out of the Garden of Eden. God even sent a cherub to guard the garden so they wouldn't be able to come back into the abundance of Eden. Didn't that seem too much? They realized their mistake and felt sorry, didn't they? Why did God have to kick them out—it was just one mistake!

If we stop there, we may be tempted to think that God was too harsh in His discipline. But if we look closer, God was actually guarding them. In the garden, there were two trees – the tree of the knowledge of good and evil (the forbidden fruit of which Adam and Eve ate, causing the fall of men), and the tree of life (Genesis 2:8-9). The tree of life would give them everlasting life. When God forbade Adam and Eve to enter the garden after the fall, He actually intervened on their behalf to prevent them from eating of the tree of life; otherwise, they would have remained cursed forever.

In the same way, we may have experienced being frustrated or offended by God's actions. We may have jumped to our conclusions about Him as a father to us. We may have felt doubts about His being tender and forgiving.

But, God, in the omnipotence of His ways, will at all times have a good reason for His actions. We can trust that those reasons are for our own good—so much so that He calls Himself love.

In embracing this truth, we can stop calculating God's deeds. We can avoid comparing ourselves to those who have been "more blessed" than we are. We can forego our self-righteousness that makes us think God prefers us over those we disapprove of. From there, the foundation of our trust and love for God would shift from His deeds to His very blameless nature. There is nothing bad or angry or spiteful about Him, and in that reassuring fact, we can find peace.

When we have that view of God, it is very hard to question and to take offense of His actions. The way His hands move no longer confounds us, and we end up finding ourselves witnesses and recipients to the perfect benevolence of His heart. It is there that we can find the confidence to say that it is His will to bless us.

SECOND CHANCES

Do you have issues in your past that bog you

down in the present?

Do you walk around carrying stigma from past mistakes?

Have people's words felt like brands on your forehead?

Are you misunderstood?

Humiliated?

Do you wish you could erase the past? Do you want a second chance?

A clean slate?

Sometimes people remember all the wrong things we have committed for a lifetime, but forget all the right things we have done in the blink of an eye. Sometimes we believe how people judge us, or we also judge ourselves and put on our own marks of condemnation.

God does not see us that way. He sees us with eyes of forgiveness, acceptance, and love. He values us not for the things we have done or have failed to do, but for who we are—His children.

When Adam, Eve, Cain, or whoever else made a mistake, God could have wiped them out instantly. He could have started over and created perfect creatures incapable of sin or failure. But He did nothing of that sort because He believes in second chances. He knows how to forget the past.

If you believe in Him, He believes in you so much more. He believes that the dreams He put in your heart can come to pass. He has placed a price tag on you that costs so much more than what you think you're worth – priceless! That is how much your Maker values you.

With this kind of love, second chances are not hard to get.

If you have never experienced the love of God, then this is an invitation for you to open your heart to Him. His arms are open wide to receive you, here and now.

If you already know of that exceptional encounter, then I invite you to dig deeper in the wells of His love. From there, allow a new level of friendship and intimacy with God to spring forth to a level where you are so utterly intoxicated by Him, that the mystery of His ways makes perfect sense, and the miracles of heaven start to infiltrate your life.

A Moment with Daddy God

*God in heaven, y*ou are a gracious and loving Father to me. I want to know your heart, to understand and experience the depths of your affections toward me. Reveal to me more of your Fatherly love, so that I may revel in its goodness. Thank you for forgiving me and seeing me to be of priceless value, for regarding me as your child! I declare that the only label I will carry is the one bearing your Name. Give me a new heart and a new perspective! Give me a heart like yours, Daddy God, for I want to be just like you. Amen and amen!

CHAPTER FIVE

Face to Face

My daily devotion time with God is precious. It is like a lifeline I need to connect with to make the most of my day. During one of these devotions, I felt something urging me to read the book of Job. This book isn't exactly the easiest book to meditate on; in fact, I think it is one of the most sorrowful and frightening stories in the Bible! Yet, within its pages lies something very valuable.

For starters, Job was a godly, blameless man who was highly favored by God. The first part of his story is an elaborate account of his wealth – livestock, servants, farmhands, properties – all of which made him the most affluent man in the area. Yet, after this account of extraordinary assets, the narrative shifts to a scene in heaven during an assembly of God's angels. Here, Satan appeared and had his conversation with God (Job 1:7-12, TNIV):

> *[7] The Lord said to Satan, "Where have you come from?" Satan answered the Lord, "From roaming through the earth and going back and forth in it" [8] Then the Lord said to Satan, "have you considered by servant Job? There is no one on earth like him; he is blameless and upright, a man who fears God and shuns evil.? [9] "Does Job fear God for nothing?", Satan replied. [10] "Have*

you not put a hedge around him and his household and everything he has? You have blessed the work of his hands, so that his flocks and herds are spread throughout the land. ¹¹But stretch out your hand and strike everything he has, and he will surely curse you to your face." ¹²The Lord said to Satan, "Very well, then, everything he has is in your hands, but on the man himself do not lay a finger." Then Satan went out from the presence of the Lord.

Not long after this happened, misfortune started to creep into Job's life. One regular day, Job found himself suddenly seized by a barrage of devastating reports:

Servant 1 (tripping over his own feet): Job, my Master, the Sabeans raided your land, stole oxen and donkeys, and killed all the farmhands!

Servant 2 (scurrying before servant 1 finished): Job, Job! A fire burned all your sheep and shepherds!

Servant 3 (running, seconds later): The Chaldeans stole your camels and killed your servant!

Servant 4 (pale, not far behind): Master, a mighty

wind caused your house to cave in. All your children are dead!

Job had 7,000 sheep, 3,000 camels, 500 yokes of oxen, 500 donkeys, hundreds of servants, and 10 children. In the blink of an eye, it was as if a celestial torrent swept away everything he owned and cherished. Job's life was turned upside down faster than he could even catch his breath.

How's that for a reflective meditation? I could not begin to imagine Job's anguish. Upon hearing this news, Job stood up and tore his robes in grief. He shaved his head and fell to the ground. Yet, amazingly, it was not in resentment and anger against God that he did this, but in worship (v. 20-21). By keeping himself from being offended by God, Job passed the first test with flying colors. However, his ordeal was far from over.

Meanwhile in heaven, another conversation took place between Satan and God. This time, Job's second test was an affliction to his physical health.

From then on, Job's body was covered with boils, from head to toe. Such was his suffering that he sat in the ashes, using a piece of broken pottery to scrape his sores. Even in his sleep Job did not find comfort, for even in the night hours he was shattered with terrifying visions (Job 7:14). It is a mystery how he kept himself sane.

The next thirty chapters of the book of Job narrate the dialogue between Job and three of his friends who came to share his grief. Their supposed act of brotherly sympathy, however, eventually turned sour and instead of encouraging Job, they started to question his faith. They falsely accused him of sin and said that he deserved his ordeal.

Job lamented over his situation and wished he were dead, cursing the day he was formed in his mother's womb. He cried out to God, without ever indicting Him. He pleaded his case before heaven because he knew he was a righteous man, and he had great confidence in his own blamelessness. Naturally, Job's claims ensued condemning rebukes from his friends who deemed him arrogant for justifying himself before God.

After a series of speeches and stressful debates with his friends, Job decided to present his case before the Lord Himself. He boldly defended his innocence and pleaded to be released from his suffering.

He protested and dared heaven to weigh his deed on scales of justice to prove his integrity. He said he would wear the allegation against him like a crown, because in his virtuousness he would appear as a prince (Job 31:36-37).

Pause.

A whirlwind appeared.

From it, the resonating voice of the Lord answered Job.

FACE TO FACE WITH ALMIGHTY GOD

We would think that the voice came to comfort Job, or maybe apologize for inflicting pain on someone as godly as he was. We would even think that the Lord came to explain to Job why he was suffering all these unbearable torments.

God didn't.

The Lord came to challenge Job, soliciting, *"Who is this that questions my wisdom with such ignorant words? Brace yourself like a man for I have some questions for you..."* (Job 38:2-3a).

Scary.

I envision that Job, festering with boils all over his body, shook as he saw the whirlwind. And hearing the Almighty challenge him, I could imagine the terror that gripped him and momentarily made him forget his maladies.

God asked Job many questions, the answers to which surely no man could provide: *"Where were you when I laid the foundations of the earth?...Where does light come from, and where does darkness go? ...Does the rain have a father? Who gives birth to the dew?"*

God challenged Job—*"Have you ever commanded the morning to appear and cause the dawn to rise in the east?...Have you ever explored the springs from which the seas come?...Do you still want to argue with the Almighty?"*

You are God's critic, but do you have the answers?

Job was rendered speechless. In this brief but thundering discourse with God, Job realized the bottom line—that God's wisdom was matchless and that there was absolutely nothing anyone could do to stop Him. Job realized that it was foolish of Him to question God's ways. If there was any comfort that He received from God, it was not that His sufferings would soon end. Rather, it was that God was in control. With that heart-stopping realization, Job's faith grew, and he knew that no matter how horrendous his situation was, he was in good hands.

THE BIGGER PICTURE

An encounter with God like this is surely extraordinary. Imagine pouring out your heart to God, and you suddenly hear an audible voice call out to you. I'm sure just the sound of it would jolt enough electricity through our veins and make your hair stand on end!

So envision how Job must have felt when God not only showed Himself, but also started to give an astonishing description of His works, as though His presence wasn't overwhelming enough. God kept elucidating the extent of His power to Job until finally Job said:

"I had only heard about You before, but now I

have seen You with my own eyes. I take back everything I said, and I sit in the dust and ashes to show my repentance." (Job 42:5-6).

He could no longer take it. Job was so utterly besieged by the presence of God that his once vociferous claims of innocence now seemed like pitiful whimpers against the immense wisdom of God.

He saw his life in the light of God's infinite plan, and there his eyes were opened.

In his previous life of bounty, Job savored the physical blessings that came from the hand of God. But it was at this lowest point of his life that he received something better – he caught a glimpse of the kind, wise, and irreproachable God first hand. As if scales had been taken from his eyes, Job realized he was not merely a recipient of God's goodness. He was, in fact, the very object God had chosen to display His sovereignty! This newfound consciousness was more than enough to erase all his queries; this realization silenced all his apprehensions.

Like what He did to Job, God sometimes brings us into situations that we do not understand. Many times these problems are so overwhelming that they cloud our vision. Everything we do is seen in the light of these trials, and because we hurt, everything that happens to us seems like salt rubbed in our wounds.

Job's story clearly tells us that God's ways are higher than our own. In His preeminence, the answer that He provides us does not always come in the form of a solution or an end to our problems. Sometimes, God answers by showing us the *bigger picture* and giving us an avenue through which our faith can grow.

FRIEND OF JOB, FRIEND OF GOD

Now that God had answered Job's complaints with a view-altering challenge, let us take a look at how He addressed Job's three reproving friends. In the last chapter of the book of Job, it says that God was angry at them for not speaking accurately about Him. God told them,

> *"...take seven bulls and seven rams and go to my servant Job and offer a burnt offering for yourselves. My servant Job will pray for you, and I will accept his prayer on your behalf..."* (Job 42:8a).

Something bizarre had just taken place. Job's

three friends had sinned against God. God was expressing His anger towards them, and He said that He would be appeased only if they brought an offering to *Job*. To Job!

Covered with boils, devastated, and alienated, Job had passed his test. As a reward, he was elevated to a place of honor before God. Prior to Job's trial, God was pleased with his devotion. Now that Job had rightly persisted in righteousness and faith the midst of affliction, God trusted Job. God trusted him so greatly that He put the fate of his three friends in his hands.

But the story does not end there. One more quality that we have to admire about Job is that he knew how to go the extra mile. When he was still rich, he would burn offerings to God, and do an extra offering for his kids just in case they forgot about a sin they might have committed.

Now, God provided Job a chance to go the extra mile again, and surely he was up to it. **Not only did Job forgive and intercede for his friends, he blessed them as well** (Job 42:10). This act of blessing releases great power.

Just as God presented Cain a mark of protection in spite of his sin, God was now allowing Job to partake of this good and godly nature by blessing the people who had sinned against him. It is one thing to overlook an offense; it is another to offer a precious gift such as a blessing to an offender. To forgive and to bless releases the divine destiny over a person's life; it is an act of God, nothing short of pure love.

THE REWARD OF BLESSING

The moment Job blessed his friends, God not only restored Job's fortunes, but wonderfully offset his extra mile by doubling it! In all, 14,000 sheep, 6,000 camels, 1,000 teams of oxen, 1,000 female donkeys, seven more sons, and three more daughters with matchless beauty, were given back to Job. These were exactly double of what Job had before.

For the next one hundred and forty years, Job would see four happy generations of his offspring. Job died an old man who had lived a long, full life. What a great way to pass on—an old man who had lived a long, full life. No regrets, no bitterness or anger, but just a serene calm that reflected a life well lived.

Job's story teaches us that greater blessings await us when, in the midst of persecution or offense, we choose to forgo the nagging desire for justice, and, in its place, offer an impartial love.

In the life of Job, the faith and dependence developed through trials and testing increased his capacity to receive. Seeing past offense, he loosened his grip on the need for revenge and now had both hands free to receive double of what he was able to hold before. Job got the greater blessing - the literal double portion.

RE-DIGGING JOB'S TREASURE

When God restored Job, he was no longer known to be the great man from the east, for he had then become the greatest. But Job's fortune was not merely his material blessings. His treasure has lived on today, a treasure that we can all enjoy and benefit from. These are what I like to call nuggets of Kingdom Truths—revelations that are as valid and valuable today as they were thousands of years ago.

As I read and studied Job's story, a powerful revelation ignited a fresh move of the Holy Spirit in my life and in our church. As children of God, we have a life of blessing mapped out before us. But we need divine desperation to live out this life of blessing. And we can lead people to this life by declaring the truth and promises of God over them.

The story of Job sheds light on another important aspect of living out this life of blessing—our relationships with God and man. I believe there is no human life sheltered enough as to have never experienced hurt. From little remarks that hurt us, to devastating betrayals and physical pain, we have seen them all. At one point or another, we have been scarred.

We are not in control of these painful situations; they just happen. But what we do have control over is how we react to these situations. When people hurt us, we can either hold a grudge or choose to walk the spiritual extra mile by both forgiving and blessing those who have wronged us. Sometimes the only thing standing between you and your next miracle is that prayer of blessing.

While God does not desire for us to have enemies, hurtful people and situations can serve as an exercise for our capacity to receive God's blessing. When seeds of anger, bitterness, or resentment are planted in our hearts, God cannot wholly occupy these. If we do not let go of these offenses, we will never be able to contain His full blessing no matter how abundant His love may be. We need to forgive and choose to go beyond the pain by offering our blessing.

It takes a friend of God to restore others to a right standing before God.

When Job prayed for his friends, they received forgiveness. But it was Job, who blessed in the midst of anguish, received the greater portion of blessings.

THE PATH TO GREATER BLESSING

I believe that sometimes God brings us into certain situations—opportunities, whereby He can teach us how to be more like Himself.

If you have been wronged and know that you have not been fully restored from it, I encourage you to pour out your heart and release that burden to Him. Let us remember that God did not allow for us to be hurt so we would suffer. Rather, God consents to situations that can lead us to face-to-face encounters with Him. For it is in these God encounters that we unearth the path to greater blessing.

While the path to forgiveness may be tough for many, the trail to forgetting may be almost impossible for some. Certain memories may cut too deep to put out of our minds, but it is not impossible. God knows that. He knows that you, too, can do more than just pardon or absolve.

A heart that is willing to let go, to pardon, to extend a hand of reconciliation, to restore, to take the high road is like an enormous spotlight demanding God's attention.

You can become the very key by which blessing and favor are unleashed in your life and in the life of others.

Like Job, let us thus seek an audience with God. He is the God whose infinite goodness we cannot contain. He is the God whose will, if received with open hands, will compel us to not just forgive, but also to spill over with a love that does not rest until it finds another to bless.

A Moment with the Omniscient God

God, you are in control. Your thoughts are so much higher than my thoughts, and I trust that I am always in good hands when I am surrendered to you. Lord, today I choose to see past all offenses. I release forgiveness to those who have hurt me in any way. Lord, I bless these people. Today I will stop hindering the flow of blessing in my life and in the life of others. I speak blessing to those who have wronged me. I declare that your Holy Spirit move them and lead them to a place of reconciliation with you. May I grow in wisdom and intimacy with you. Help me make it a lifestyle to extend and release blessings to others.

CHAPTER SIX

Marking Others

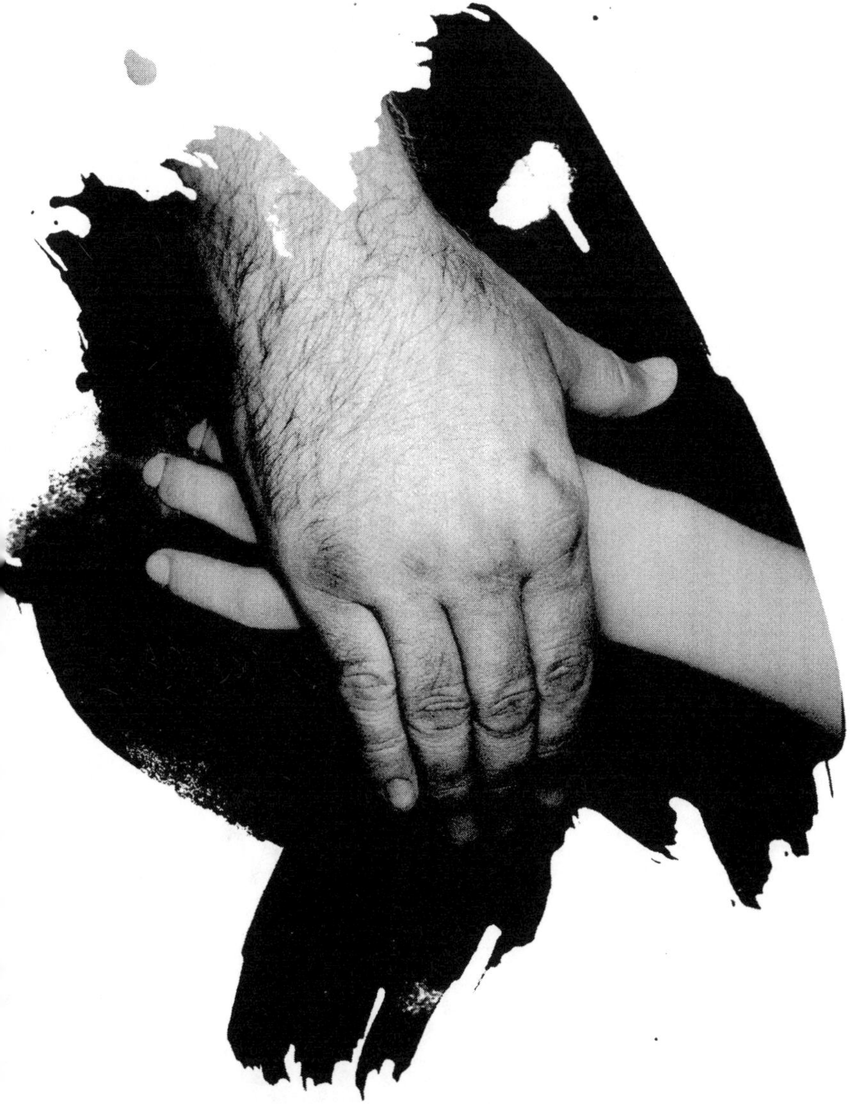

As human beings we live by certain laws of nature. Laws of science describe how things work. The law of gravitation tells us why things fall back to the earth when we throw them up towards the sky. The law of attraction tells us that "likes" attract each other – the reason why we have cliques and friends with similar interests. The law of supply and demand explains why almost anyone can buy salt with their coins, but only people like computer mogul Bill Gates can buy diamonds with his bills.

Take for example an electric socket. Why shouldn't we stick knives and forks in wall sockets? Only those who understand electricity know. A person with understanding knows that the same electricity he uses to cook his eggs every morning, could burn his house down if misused. He abides by the laws of electricity and uses them to his advantage.

As individuals, I think at one point or another we all make 'laws' to manage and direct ourselves. We give ourselves deadlines to do well on the job, weight limits to look good in the mirror, and bed times to be alert the next day. When we don't know and follow certain rules, we become frenzied. But when our knowledge of these 'laws' are grounded and practiced, our lives and society take shape.

Similarly, the Kingdom of God operates based on certain laws and principles. One of the most basic, yet, oftentimes, overlooked principles is that **things are said, declared, and pronounced before they come into being.**

We see this principle in action even in the first chapter of the first book of the Bible, Genesis 1.

> *"Then God said, 'Let there be light,' and there was light."* (v. 3)
>
> *"Then God said, 'Let there be a space between the waters, to separate the waters of the heavens from the waters of the earth.' And that is what happened."* (v.6)

And the rest of creation goes on, with God's words commanding things into existence.

This principle can be seen in action at various times in the Bible. Adam's first assignment as governor of creation was to name the animals. Whatever animal God brought to him, Adam named the animal, and that was its name (Genesis 2:19). What a scene it must have been—all the world's animals lining up for a census with Adam calling out their names: Panda! Chameleon! Turtle! Bobcat! These animals had already existed and were essentially roaming about the earth, yet they were in lack. **It was only when man called out each creature's name that the fullness of their identities were achieved.**

Another occasion when the principle of *'saying, declaring, and pronouncing'* was practiced is in Acts 3. Peter and John were going to the temple to pray when a crippled man begged them for money. Instead of offering money, Peter and John looked at him and said, *"Silver or gold I do not have, but what I have I give you. In the name of Jesus Christ of Nazareth, walk!"* The beggar then got up and started to walk...and leap! He pleaded for alms, but Peter and John offered something far better—they declared healing and directed heaven to send the miracle.

The man's situation turned because the apostles commanded a blessing to come upon him. From these few examples, one of the bylaws of the Kingdom becomes clear: **words have power and when released, they create a significant change.**

THE WORD OF HIS POWER

The spoken word is a potent and deliberate force.

God designated the spoken word as the vehicle for the release of His power. Through God's utterance, enough power was released to create the earth and everything in it—all creatures big and small, living and inanimate.

But when it was time for God to create man, when He had formed His masterpiece from clay into His image, why did He NOT speak to it? It was because man is so special that God, Himself, breathed life into man's form.

It was for man that God spoke all other things into being, so that man can live in abundance while enjoying boundless fellowship with God. And the power of His spoken word did not cease when creation concluded. To this very day, God speaks so that all things can be sustained. Hebrews 1:3 says:

"And He is the radiance of His glory and the exact representation of His nature, and [He] **upholds all things by the word of His power...**" (NASB, emphasis mine)

God upholds all things by the power of His words. His word is so powerful that it maintains creation to this very day. It is through His words that prevent the earth from tilting even a degree more than it should; keeps the boundaries of land and sea; and commands the sun to rise and set, just as He did when He first created the earth. But there is more!

With His power, God not only upholds creation, but with it, He maintains the entire blessing He meant for us to have when He first created Adam and Eve.

In each person remains a dormant seed of the abundance God originally intended for us to have before the fall of man!

We may struggle to believe that in us there lays a budding destiny of an abundant life, just waiting to sprout and manifest itself. Many of us may live a life that is a far cry from the carefree and contented life that Adam was meant to live. But allow me to illustrate my point with a simple question:

Does a fruitless mango tree lie when he says he is a mango tree?

No, because he is still a mango tree regardless of whether or not he is bearing fruit! So even if we live the most boring, monotonous, frustrating, or disgruntled life in the world, we still have the potential to live out a life of blessing and a great God-given destiny. That potential may be hidden and inactive at the moment, but it can surely be released!

THE WORD ON WINGS

Spoken words are empowered when those who hear them believe in them!

When the enemy came to tempt Adam and Eve in the garden, he used crafty words to turn their hearts from God. But the temptation itself did not defile Adam and Eve. It was after believing Satan's corruption and acting on it that they fell into the sin that separated them from God.

The power of God's words transcends time and space. Mark 8 tells the story of a centurion who once asked Jesus to heal his servant. Seeing the man's despair, Jesus replied, "I will go and heal him." In faith, the centurion countered, "Lord, I do not deserve to have You come under my roof. But just say the word, and my servant will be healed..." (v. 8). Amazed at the centurion's confidence,

Jesus said, "Go! Let it be done just as you believed it would." And the servant was healed at that moment (v. 13).

Spoken words take wings and transform the circumstances of those who hear them and respond in faith! This is law of the Kingdom of God; it is how things work in His realm!

DECREEING CHANGE

In any kingdom, from the ancient times of King Solomon to the modern monarchies of Brunei, Saudi Arabia, and Swaziland, a King (or Queen) rules by decree. The ruler's authority and the manifestation of his governance are preceded either by his personal orders or through the pronouncements of men in his regime. In the same way, when Jesus commissioned his twelve disciples to spread the Word of God, he sent them out with these instructions (Matthew 10:6-7, NIV, emphasis mine):

> "*⁶...Go rather to the lost sheep of Israel. ⁷As you go, proclaim this message: 'The kingdom of heaven has come near.'*"

Jesus Christ sent these men on a mission to change the world. He granted them **authority,** which they were to administer through the **proclamation** of the message of the Kingdom.

In the New Testament, we read testimonies of how the disciples, who were dedicated servant-leaders in their own rights, used their words and declarations to shape the spiritual atmosphere of every place they set their feet upon.

They healed the sick.

They cast out demons.

They raised the dead.

They changed the lives of multitudes.

But they did none of these extraordinary things with their own human efforts.

The twelve disciples were ordinary people who were able to perform miracles because they contained the heavenly authority given to them by Jesus. They, in turn, conveyed this power through their words.

MARKING OTHERS WITH BLESSING

Just as Jesus instructed his disciples to proclaim the Kingdom of God, we too have the responsibility to be stewards of the power He bestowed upon us the moment we accepted Him as our Lord and Savior. We are to bring the Kingdom, which entails righteousness, peace, and joy, into our homes and societies.

One way we can bring God's Kingdom on earth is by marking people with blessing—by verbally declaring the will of God to be fulfilled in people's lives and circumstances.

The Hebrew word for blessing is *beraka*, which literally means 'the giving of the power and favor of God.' When we pronounce blessing on someone in Jesus' name, we are actually commanding the power and favor of God to move in their lives—to strengthen discouraged hearts, to heal the sick, to create peace, to reverse dire circumstances, and even to call out the great destiny that lies dormant in them.

God created the world through His words, and with our own; we co-labor with Him by making it a better one.

Before God spoke the world into being, it was a formless mass. There was no hint of lush forests or vibrant creatures. Yet He spoke to the nothingness and called out its destiny—to be a planet of life and robustness. In the same way, we should not let grim situations stop us from seeing and calling out what could be a glorious scenario.

Just as a fruitless mango tree possesses the seed and potential to bear mango fruit, so every person has within them the promise of an abundant life in Christ, no matter his or her circumstances. When spreading the Kingdom, let us not look at people according to what their circumstances paint them to be. Rather, let us see them the way God envisioned them to be when He first drew their images in His heart. And let us do the same for ourselves!

Whenever we verbally declare blessings, we call forth this divine image and the fullness of every blessing that comes along with it.

Being led by the Holy Spirit, we see the promising future and prophesy it to happen in the now. Operating by the law of the Kingdom, we shape what is unseen; we make tangible what is impossible; and we transform what is hopeless through the power of our words and our faith in the God who hears them. David's great triumph over Goliath sprouted as he burned with holy indignation. Goliath taunted the Israelites and so, before the Israeli army, David bravely declared to King Saul in 1 Samuel 17:36-37:

> *"Your servant has killed both the lion and the bear; this uncircumcised Philistine will be like one of them, because he has defied the armies of the living God. The LORD who rescued me from the paw of the lion and the paw of the bear will rescue me from the hand of this Philistine."*

Then facing Goliath, David defiantly declared (1 Samuel 17:46-47, TNIV):

> *"This day the LORD will deliver you into my hands, and I'll strike you down and cut off your head...All those gathered here will know that it is not by sword or spear that the LORD saves; for the battle is the LORD's, and he will give all of you into our hands."*

What boldness! From David, we learn that we **can only seize in the physical what we first see with our spiritual eyes**.

I have seen a similar faith from a theatrically inclined faculty member of a University in my hometown. Let's call him Carlo. Though very successful in his career, he had struggles with his identity and in finding meaning in the things he did. While doing research for a play that played around a Christian theme, he decided to attend the Condensed World Missions Course offered in our church. He clearly did not know what he was in for!

It was during the graduation of this course that I first prayed for Carlo. I prayed and declared that he would be propelled into his destiny. Nothing happened overnight, but I continued to meet with him for personal discipleship. I kept declaring that his life would be a vessel for God's glory.

Through the next several months, Carlo's views started to change and he began to see how his life could bring glory to God. From a man unsure of his purpose, he became purpose-driven and even more passionate for his craft. His play gathered great reviews in the local national newspapers. This caught the attention of a provincial Governor, who then commissioned him to do a production to promote the region's ecotourism.

Afterwards, Carlo was able to direct another major play, and in the same year he was selected as one of the Philippines' 21 Emerging Leaders Awardees. But the blessings were just starting to pour forth! The following year, the University honored Carlo with the Outstanding Creative Artist award. With the cash prize he received, Carlo decided to attend a cultural exposure overseas. During his nine months there, he was able to pull off a multicultural, multilingual, and multimedia theatre production with many international artists. What a turnaround!

The greatest of blessings, however, were the changes I saw in Carlo's life. His perspective changed. He became more accepting and loving. He became more ardent in articulating the needs of artists like himself. As the days passed, Carlo found himself, yet again, overcome with blessing. He received an Asian Artists' Grant funded by a prestigious foundation to pursue a Masters in Fine Arts in Directing. As a scholar, he became privileged to do his internship at a prominent theater company in the United States. With his life in tune with God's purpose, Carlo saw his life change in ways he could not have imagined before.

Another story is that of a woman named Maria

who owned a restaurant business. She heard me testify about the breakthroughs among our church members and encouraging those who hear the testimonies to claim them as their own. And she did just that!

Let me give a brief background of Maria's situation. A rival restaurant that had just set up shop right next to their building was threatening their family business. Her son was undergoing depression and even suicidal tendencies after breaking up with his girlfriend who had just miscarried his baby.

Maria approached me after that worship service and asked me fervently to pray for her. She said that she would not let me go until I blessed her! Oh what a good heart! So ferocious in faith, yet so humble before God. So, I said a prayer of blessing and declared new clarity and direction in her life. I also declared a breakthrough in their family business. When Maria got home that night, she prayed over her son who was then fast asleep.

Not long afterwards, Maria's life and family situation started to change. Her son started to live his life again—he got a haircut, went to the gym, learned to drive, and re- enrolled in school. Their restaurant started to pick up, and in just a few months, they were able to renovate. A mall concessionaire awarded them, and their catering services grew such that they began supplying food for a thriving resort. Before the year ended, Maria also got a new car.

Maria was hungry for God to move in her life. This made her a target, not only of His blessing, but of His favor, as well.

The last story is about a teacher and musician named Don. Don grew up in a family that practiced the occult. Young and rebellious, he would get into fist fights. After being jailed, at one point, because of his aggression, he was sent to a far-flung province to continue his secondary education.

In college, he channeled his anger towards getting good grades and being a better man, especially when he married his pregnant girlfriend. But he hit rock bottom when he found out that his wife got pregnant again, by another man. Outraged and betrayed, he wanted to commit suicide. By God's grace, Don found himself kneeling in prayer instead, desperate to see hope beyond his situation.

Soon afterwards, a couple reached out to Don and his wife and shared the Good News. Their relationship slowly started to heal, but it was an uphill struggle, and they eventually agreed to separate. Don entrusted his daughter to his brother's family while he worked in Manila (the capital city), three hours away. It was while he was looking for a job closer to home that I met him at a birthday party of a common friend. I said a short prayer for his needs.

Gradually, his life began to be restored. Hired as a faculty member of a public university, he could now be with his daughter. He rendered outstanding performances in concerts, and he also released an album. Because of his renewed vigor as a teacher and artist, Don received a scholarship to pursue graduate studies in one of the universities in the United States.

SPURRING ACTION

Marking people for blessing is not a magic formula that we can use to create something out of nothing in the snap of a finger. The words we utter can only fulfill the purposes of God if they are directed by Him and aligned with His intentions.

In spreading the Kingdom, we should remember to speak words as a prayer declaration or prophecy. These spoken words stir up faith from the hearer that, in turn, spurs His action.

David did not kill Goliath by merely describing Goliath's death. With a mighty working of the Spirit of God, he slew the giant with his sling and a stone.

The principle of faith, declaration, and action is true in our lives. We cannot stop tempestuous storms simply by describing sunny weather; we cannot deal with lack by explaining wealth. Instead, we place our trust in the God who controls the times and seasons of life, and, in faith, anticipate His reply.

Not all Goliaths may be slain, and not all problems may be solved the way we expect them to be. But in any case, good will always come out of a heart filled with faith.

If things turn for the better we praise God; if they don't, then we still praise Him. In this process, David-like hearts will be fashioned, and indignant and bitter hearts will begin to be shaped for the purposes of God.

SEE IT, SAY IT

Wrapping up, I am reminded of Adam in the Garden of Eden naming the animals God paraded before him. Here, the animals existed in bodily forms, but their essence was only realized when Adam called out their names.

When we are in the presence of God, He sometimes parades blessings before our eyes. In intimate times with the Lord, He rouses dreams and desires in us that cannot be accomplished by our earthly flesh.

Instead, His Spirit bids us to call out those blessings and declare what the eyes of our faith have seen into reality. In this realm there are no limitations to how big or how great a blessing could be. **The only limitation that exists is our capacity to see what He sees.** Thankfully, we can develop that ability to see as we spend more and more time with Him.

Creation groans for the manifestation of the sons of God. The bleak world and the people around us are needy for the glory intended for them since the beginning of time. As children of God, we have been entrusted with the capacity to effect change and steward people back into the heavenly course by our actions and declarations.

Marking people with blessing is an important Kingdom principle. The more we practice it, the more we become aware of its outcomes. The more outcomes we see, the more our faith will grow. Then one day we will realize that we, ourselves, have become the very target of the change we created – we become more and more like the person God intended us to be: marked with blessing and all geared up to bless others

A Moment with the King of Kings

Dear Lord, your Word is so rich and so powerful. Thank you for revealing precious truths about your Kingdom. Help us to remember and grow in these revelations, Lord. When we see people in need, use us to speak to their lives so that their faith may grow and they will receive their breakthroughs. Give us your wisdom to speak the right Words, with a right heart. We desire to be hearers, bearers, and spreaders of your Word. We open ourselves to the working of your Holy Spirit, in order to grow deeper and deeper in intimacy with you so that we may bless you and be a blessing to others. Amen.

CHAPTER SEVEN

Blessed

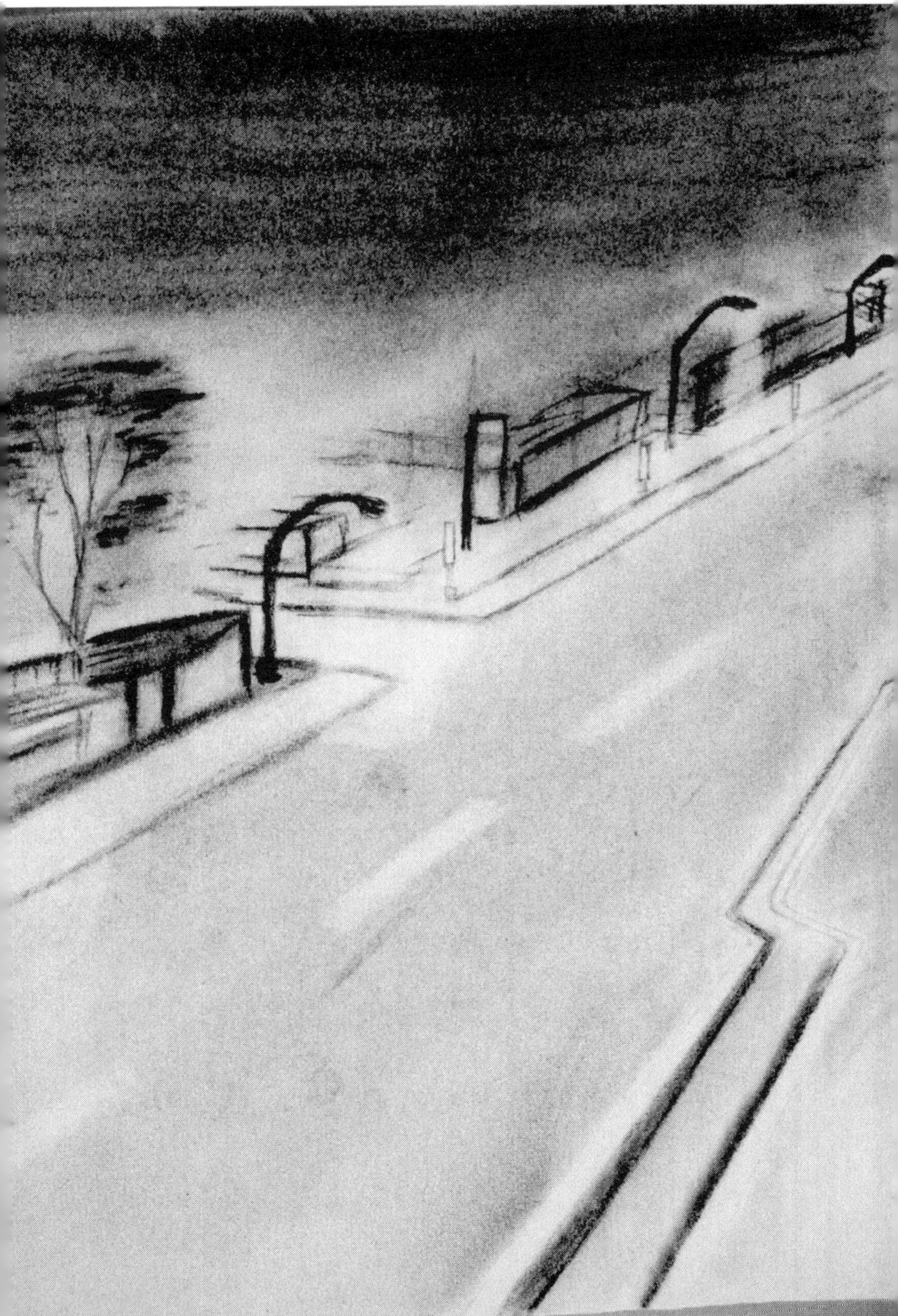

What does a perfect world look like to you?

World peace? No sickness, suffering, or strife? Money growing on trees and beach houses on sale for 100 bucks? Five-day weekends and two-day workdays?

In a perfect world, our hair would never thin out and people would always be optimistic, without knowledge of dishonesty, disillusionment, or disaster whatsoever.

The Bible paints its own picture of a perfect world. In the beginning of time, when man freely fellowshipped with God, when abundance was the byword of the world, and when Adam and Eve knew only of the beautiful.

Let us take one more journey and delve into the world they lived in. Let us take a good look at what this life of perfect favor looks like and what it means to be blessed, in a place of blessing.

EDEN REVISITED

God made the Garden of Eden after He created Adam.

At this time, God had already created all types of vegetation—plants, trees, moss, and fungi. He had also created the animals of the earth, sky, and seas. Yet, amidst this idyllic landscape of glory and abundance, God made another special place where man would dwell, the Garden.

If we read the book of Genesis carefully, we can see that before God breathed life into man, all the earth's vegetation did not yet bear fruit:

"When the Lord God made the earth and the heavens, neither wild plants nor grains were growing on the earth. For the Lord God had not yet sent rain to water the earth, and there were no people to cultivate it." (Genesis 2:4-5, NLT)

Why was the earth unproductive? First, because God had not yet sent rain, and more importantly, because there were no people to cultivate it. Reading further into Genesis chapter 2 (v. 15):

"The Lord God placed the man in the Garden of Eden to tend and watch over it." (NLT, emphasis mine).

The Garden of Eden, in all its abundance, was not handed to Adam on a silver platter. **Man was not a pet to be fed, but an able-bodied being capable of gathering food. Man is competent and responsible enough to govern over everything that God has created.**

Many of us think that before the fall of man, everything was free and nothing had to be worked on. Everything was perfectly wonderful. We think what Adam and Eve did all day was to laze around, gaze at clouds, and walk with God in the dirt paths of the beautiful garden.

But Genesis 2 tells us otherwise. Since the beginning, God had designed man to co-labor with Him. God held back the rain and the trees did not bear fruit until man was around to till the land. The difference is, in that place of blessing, before the fall of man, labor was not synonymous with toil.

Labor was fulfilling and enjoyable, because everything Adam set his hands to bore fruit.

Everything he planted grew, prospered, and multiplied. Adam was blessed by God and the more he operated with God, the more his dwelling became a place of blessing. Adam was relishing his destiny in Eden—His efforts were offset by God's generosity and all of Heaven's favor was directed at him, like a giant spotlight that magnified and followed his every move. Such was the perfect world God had intended for mankind to live in.

EDEN RESTORED

Eden was a literal garden with trees, animals, flowers, and green grass. Yet, I picture it more like a lush forest than a quaint little garden, much like the National Parks we have today, albeit more diverse and pristine. The difference with Eden is that it was made for man. Vegetation covered the earth even before Adam was created, but Eden was a gift from God, and everything in it worked for the benefit of man.

God made everything in Eden revolve around man, its governor. It was a place of abundance, peace, love, harmony, joy, and restoration. It was a place where every good and perfect gift from God was made available for man.

Eden was where God placed the sinless man. Eden is a picture of our destiny in God. Destiny

is where the best you, the you that is perfected by Grace, will flourish.

The best you is the one that has encountered the extraordinary God. Hence, you have been permanently ruined for an ordinary, monotonous life.

The physical Garden of Eden may not exist today, but its essence still remains in the perfect will of God for us. In His heart, Eden is still gloriously alive. When we abandon all else to pursue the things of His heart, all of Eden is made available to us.

In Hebrew the name Eden means *pleasure* or *delight*. The Garden is a place where you can experience not only the love, but also the delight the Father has for you. It is the place where you can clearly see that the favor of God is not based on merit, but based on the overflow of His faultless heart.

If you look deep into God's heart, you will see that He does not just settle for you, He is happy with you.

Where you are now, what you are going through, are all parts of a grand plan. You are exactly where God wants you to be.

It doesn't matter if you are a robber, cheater, adulterer, or any other unholy character. For sinners and saints alike, He bought you with His own blood because He wants you. He wants you with a reckless, forceful love that flattens every unworthy human cell and turns it into a mound of grace-dependent, God-praising flesh that spends the day in awe of the goodness of the Father.

So what does your Eden look like?

What is that great destiny that God planned for you to live out?

What do you dream about?

I pray that these questions stir inside your heart as you meditate and feast on the reality of His affections for you. I pray that God would show you how enormous a heart He has for you.

Ask God what He was thinking when He made you. The answer might just blow you away.

What were you wired to do? Where do you function best? What field has He given you to excel in? That is your Eden and influence. In that area is where you were destined to achieve for His glory.

IN A NUTSHELL

In the last six chapters of this book, we have talked about God's mark of blessing – a seal that promises a life of supernatural favor. We have journeyed through the colossal heart of God from which this favor flows. We have seen the long hand that extends restoration to murderers and liars in the deepest pits, and comfort to the most disheartened hearts. We have peeked into the lives of men and women who have experienced Holy visitations that turned their lives right side up. We have learned that the power of God that changes dire situations lies in people who have chosen to fully surrender their lives to God. They are people who have decided to forgive, to align to His will, and to verbally pass the blessing to others so that they could, in turn, experience the same life-changing, face-to-face encounter with God.

Part I of this book puts the limelight on the goodness of God, on His intentions, and on His making us a target of blessing. Part II discusses how we can take this blessing and channel it to others. God-encounters that served as turning points and divine providence are the focus of Chapters 1 and 2. In

Chapter 3 we talked about identity and how, like Jacob, we sometimes struggle to forge who we are. We forget that we should just allow God to confront every ugly part of us and take control so that our uniqueness and best colors of our characters would be revealed. We are sons and daughters of the Almighty, and we have the inheritance of a mighty destiny.

Chapter 4, on the other hand, assures us of the unconditional and unreserved love of God our Father. Cain, despite his transgression was given a mark of protection, as were Adam and Eve when they fell into sin and were driven out of Eden. **There is no circumstance, in heaven, on earth, or below that could ever separate us from the encompassing love of God.**

In Chapter 5, we examined the life of Job and how despite all hardships, he trusted the infallible heart of God for Him. This faith led Job to receive a double portion of everything he had. His Eden, **his destiny, was not merely abundance wrought by his own hands, but abundance that was fused with the supernatural favor of God**. We run into this kind of blessing when our actions are the direct expressions of our faith, love, and dependence on God. This kind of life undoubtedly attracts God's attention and heaven's resources.

As Royals, we live out this destiny when we imitate the ways of our Father, the King, who rules by decree. We command and spread the nature of God's heavenly Kingdom when we verbally release it here on earth – by marking others with a blessing. This was explored in Chapter 6, where we also established the potency of the spoken Word and its power to release the potential in the lives of the people. Like David, we slay Goliaths when in the strength of God, we refuse to accept grim situations as is. **We overcome battles when we are convinced that what we see with our spiritual eyes have the makings of reality.**

When God called Abraham (Genesis 12), He said He would bless him. This blessing God gave Abraham is unto greatness and it comes with the rewards of God's presence, prosperity, posterity, purpose, promotion, and peace. Our stories may be different, but our God is one and the same – divinely unpredictable sometimes, but gracious and ever faithful.

A Prayer of Blessing

It is ingrained in my heart that every person who reads these stories of victory will be overcome by the Holy Spirit's moving. You are chosen; you are loved. May you be released from any hindrances in the past that have kept you bound, and in forgiveness, may you be free to experience a life of love, hope, peace, and joy.

I mark everyone who reads these words with blessing. And I declare a shift and a breakthrough upon every circumstance in your life. May you live with a new sense of purpose – to bless others, just as you have been blessed. In Jesus' name. Amen.

> **"I will make you into a great nation and I will bless you; I will make your name great, and you will be a blessing. I will bless those who bless you, and whoever curses you I will curse; and all peoples on earth will be blessed through you."**
>
> Genesis 12:2-3, TNIV

EPILOGUE

Arresting Destiny

As the wind that grazed the roof above him, he breathed deep and let the memories sweep his mind until these became so clear; they sent shivers down his spine. That night, his usually straight posture was bent, and he sat with his head in his hands. For the millionth time, he silently vowed to himself that he would make things right.

Forty years had passed since he witnessed the miracles that would forever shape him and his life. Since he was born, all he had known was a life of slavery, toil, and oppression under Egypt. But one fateful day, his people's fortunes started to change. With the sickening plagues of frogs literally falling from the sky, and insects gnawing through cattle skin making him writhe, it was the purpose behind these events that struck him the most. The distant God whom they only knew through narratives had suddenly become real, and He had his people in mind to liberate. When growls came up from the rocky depths to part the red sea, Caleb was certain that the life he had known for so long would never be the same again.

Caleb remembered how the freedom shouts of joy fainted in the distance and were gradually replaced by anxious murmurs of disorientation among the Israelites. They were free, but where they were headed was nothing more than a mirage of hope in the desert, up until his adventure began. Finally, Moses appointed him, and eleven others as spies to scout-out the land. The land was Canaan—the land that God wanted them to occupy. God promised it would be a land flowing with milk and honey. He couldn't believe the lush territory was going to be theirs.

And so Caleb, Joshua, and ten other spies entered Canaan. They spent forty days unearthing the land's treasures. Everything was in such immense proportions that even a cluster of grapes had to be carried by two full-grown men! But alas, the inhabitants of the land were equally massive—the Anakites, descendants of giants. Scared as he was, Caleb did not falter in his faith when he first saw the Anakites. How mighty and powerful His God must be, he thought, to want to deliver these giants into the hands of undersized Israelites like himself.

But as their forty days of exploration neared the end, one of the elders timidly expressed his doubt, "Is it really God's will for us to take this land? Maybe we heard wrong...there are giants here! Compared to them we are like little grasshoppers waiting to be crushed." In an instant, this little seed of hesitation lodged itself into the hearts of the mighty men. Hence, as they marched back to the Israelite camp, they brought with them a load of fear instead of visions of triumph.

Their fright grew, and with every inch, their faith diminished. In their eyes, the giants became bigger than they actually were. As they marched back to camp, they put on somber faces and hoped that the bad report they carried would cover their apparent lack of courage.

They were spotted at the outskirts of the camp. Women and children eagerly ran to them, rushing for a good spot from where they could hear about the land of milk and honey that they were soon to enter. The men showed before

Moses, Aaron, and the clans of Israel hefty clusters of grapes that attested to the bounty of Canaan.

But as they continued their account of the promise land, the crowds began to stir, and their hearts began to sink. Ten of the most influential men of Israel had returned to announce that the land God had told them to seize was fortified to the sky and guarded by a throng of Goliaths.

Knowing they had to obey God, the women started to sob, wailing because they foresaw images of their husbands and sons dying in battle, like tiny insects in the hands of cruel, hefty monsters. What God had intended to be a land of promise, they now saw as a sentence of death.

Caleb remembered that scene as if it were yesterday. Amidst the chaos, he darted a look at his friend, Joshua, and as their eyes met, they knew they were one in Spirit. He calmed the crowd, raising his voice above the mob of weeping Israelites. Then he turned to Moses and said, "Let's go at once to take the land, we can certainly conquer it!" But before he could finish, the spies hushed him and yelled, "It is impossible! They will devour us!" Feeding on each other's dismay, the weeping resumed, and the little seed of doubt that sprouted in the heart of one leader had now become a jungle of disbelief and offense in the heart of many.

Moses and Aaron fell face down on the ground as the whole of Israel accused and rebelled against them. The people plotted among themselves to choose a new leader and to go back to Egypt, their prison of oppression and slavery.

So angry were the crowds that they had to willfully stop themselves from throwing rocks at Moses for bringing them out of Egypt.

Witnessing this, Joshua and Caleb tore their clothing in despair. With all their might and tears, they tried to persuade Israel to pursue Canaan as planned, "The land we traveled through and explored is a wonderful land flowing with milk and honey! And if the Lord is pleased with us, He will hand it over to us. Do not be afraid and do not rebel against the Almighty! The giants will be our prey because the Lord is with us! The Lord is with us!"

Joshua shouted with all his might until his voice grew hoarse and was drowned by the murmurs of the incredulous mob.

"The Lord is with us," Joshua and Caleb whispered as they sat in the dust.

God was dismayed that a people whom he had delivered, cared for, and displayed His miracles to would react with such unbelief and contempt. It was an insult to His face. If it were not for His friends, Moses and Aaron, who begged Him to spare the Israelites, He would have struck them dead with a plague. In His mercy, He pardoned Israel, but as a God of justice, He swore that all those who refused His promise be taken for their word. In the Lord's presence, the ten spies who incited rebellion were doomed to death. Even before they tried to conquer the Promised Land, they fell over, diseased and dead. For each of the forty years they spent seeing, yet, denying the goodness of Canaan, the Israelites would pay with a year of wandering in the wilderness.

And now, after four decades of roaming in the desert, Caleb sat down and pondered.

Moses, Aaron, and many of the men he honored had passed away. But his life was not a complete waste, he thought, for their journey opposite of Canaan was not a boring one. He spent the years with his family, seeing his children and grandchildren grow, eating and drinking as the Lord provided.

Caleb had his share of conquests, battle scars, and victory tales over other lands. But he knew these were all passing endeavors as he had yet to enter the land of promise God had prepared for his people. With a long, deep sigh, he reminded himself, that in spite of all the 'good' he had acquired, the 'best' was still to come.

Here he was, eighty-five years old with men half his age, yet his strength and faith neither failed him. He was ready to rally.

Three days before, their leader Joshua had heard from the Lord that it was time to cross over to the Promised Land. Joshua gathered the officers of Israel and said, "You will cross the Jordan River and take possession of the land the Lord your God is giving to you! Remember the words of Moses and let us strong warriors conquer our territory!"

With a resounding shout, the valiant men of Israel heaved the blessing of heaven upon their people as they resounded, "So be it, we will do whatever you command us, and we will go wherever you send us. We will obey you as we did Moses, we will silence those who go against you, so be strong and take courage!"

At that moment, something in the heavens churned as their faith thundered louder than their voices. They marked and hedged themselves in with blessing.

There they were on the banks of the Jordan with only one thing standing in their way—a river larger and fiercer than the Red Sea. This was a dilemma much larger than the Anakites and stronger than buttressed walls. It was a tempest they had to face head-on. Their circumstances seemed grim, but Caleb and the men knew fully well that their destiny was at stake.

Caleb knew that they could either cower away, or for the second time, stare destiny in the face, grab it by the throat, and claim it as their own.

At the break of Dawn, the people gathered. In arms, priests and warriors alike, all equipped with faith and courage, stood before the Jordan and prepared to cross it. With the Ark of the Covenant in the front lines, they stepped into the tumultuous river, armed with nothing but God's favor.

The moment their sandals touched the edge of the water, the river's gush backed a great distance, flowing instead to the Dead Sea until the riverbed was dry. As the water parted beneath their feet, the history they knew as handed to them through generations – of God's mighty hand in Egypt, of the parting of the Red Sea, of the miracles in the desert—was suddenly intensified with the makings of their own story.

In all-embracing awe, they crossed into the land of promise. As they declared, so it came to pass. And Israel became a great nation, with the glory of God resting on them as their greatest treasure.

This memory played in Caleb's mind that morning as he meditated on God's goodness. There he was, standing on a hill overlooking Hebron. He gazed over his possessions, his family, and his people, and breathed a whisper of thanks.

The syllables of the name he bore: Caleb, *Keleb*, meant nothing short of a dog. But in the middle of his name were the syllables that defined him, *Leb*, meaning heart or understanding. This is the name he claimed for himself, Caleb, a man of heart and understanding.

Caleb knew that the promise God gave to Abraham was his, as well. He lived a full life. He lived a blessed life. He lived out his dream.

His story is your story, too.

You are a great nation and God blesses you; He makes your name great, and you are a blessing... all peoples on earth will be blessed through you.